Growing Australian Natives in Pots

Livistona species in a 20 cm plastic pot standing inside a cane basket. Plant has been in same container for 3 years.

Syzygium wilsonii **right** and *Hardenbergia violacea* **left** in pots supported with wire hangers shown in drawings.

GROWING AUSTRALIAN NATIVES IN POTS

Indoors & Outdoors

Alec M. Blombery

Kangaroo Press

Preface

With the increasing development of multi-residential buildings on small allotments—town houses, villa homes, home units and retirement villages—more and more people are cultivating plants in containers. A growing number of people are now enjoying one or more of their favourite native plants as potted specimens.

I first began a book on growing Australian native plants in containers in 1975 after an extended stay in Europe, where considerable use is made of potted Australian plants in botanic gardens. The project was put aside in its early stages in 1976 to allow other works on plants to be completed. I am indebted to the publisher for his request for a book on this topic, which encouraged me to complete the work.

I hope that the reader will find the book helpful and so be encouraged to further cultivation and understanding of Australian native plants.

I wish to thank Brian Walters for providing transparencies of plants in hanging baskets, friends who have allowed me to photograph specimen plants including Canberra Botanic Gardens, the Potmart, Nock & Kirby, and my wife, Marie, who has once more enabled me to produce a legible manuscript.

Alec M. Blombery
1983

Cover: *Hibbertia stellaris* (p.74)

Reprinted 1987
First published in 1983 by Kangaroo Press
3 Whitehall Road (P.O. Box 75) Kenthurst 2154
Typeset by G.T. Setters Pty Limited
Printed in Hong Kong by Colorcraft Ltd

ISBN 0 949924 69 5

Contents

1. Australian Natives as Pot Plants

Growing Australian plants as potted specimens provides almost unlimited possibilities for everyone to enjoy the cultivation of a native plant. By using correct methods, anyone living in buildings with restricted garden space, such as a home unit or even a single room, can grow a native plant as a potted specimen. They can be grown in pots, flower boxes, tubs, baskets or other forms of container to suit a particular need.

For the person with the established garden which may consist entirely of exotic species, or for the gardener who would like an additional interest, a container of some type with a selected native plant can be another feature.

It should be borne in mind that, contrary to general opinion, Australian plants have similar requirements to plants from other parts of the world, although some types are naturally more selective in their needs than others.

In this book the term "potted plant" refers to plants of various types grown in prepared soil in pots and containers of different forms, such as plastic, terracotta and cement containers, planter troughs, baskets, or other vessels in which a plant may be grown. The term also includes epiphytic plants attached to and growing on pieces of suitable material, such as pieces of tea tree branch, tree fern trunk, sawn timber, cork or even the outer surface of a terracotta pot.

Advantages and Disadvantages of Growing Plants in Containers

By growing plants in containers it is possible to provide specialised conditions which may be difficult to achieve when the plant is grown in the ground. Thus it is possible to grow successfully more selective types of plants, such as boronia, and move them indoors for short periods when in flower.

The main disadvantage of growing plants in containers is the more frequent watering required, compared with growing plants in the ground.

Plant Habitats

As Australia extends over a large area, it has a wide diversity of climate from hot and tropical zones to cool and temperate regions. Within these various zones there are varying rainfall areas, from the east coast sections of high rainfall to the very arid parts of Central Australia. This diversity has resulted in many different forms of plants, from the annuals of arid areas to the rainforest type plants of the east coast. Generally most of the small floriferous plants grow in sunny positions in soils which are low in plant nutrients.

Understanding these various factors will enable a better selection of plants. It must be borne in mind that plants from arid areas have a short life when grown in moist coastal areas. Similarly, plants from high rainfall areas do not grow successfully in dry arid zones unless a moist atmosphere can be provided. Even with the natural restrictive growth habits of some plants, it is still often worthwhile to be able to enjoy these plants from extreme areas, even if for only a limited period.

Habits of Growth

For convenience we can arrange plants into three main groups, according to the nature and habit of growth. These are: terrestrial, epiphytic and aquatic plants.

It should always be borne in mind that some types of plants, like people, are more adaptable and more robust than others, and can cope more readily with changes in their normal growth habits; likewise, there are those species which are most particular in their requirements and, unless conditions approaching those in which they normally grow are provided, poor results may be obtained.

Terrestrial Plants

As the name implies, this group of plants grow with their roots in the ground, which may be any type of soil. This group covers most of those plants which are commonly cultivated and with which we are familiar.

In their natural habitat terrestrial plants grow under a wide range of conditions, from dry arid zones to lush rainforest areas, in many different types of soil. Between these two extremes, there is an enormous diversity of conditions which influence plant growth.

Some plants grow in cool, moist, sandy locations, others in half shade, some in dry locations, some in boggy places; generally most of the free-flowering species are found where there is ample sunlight.

A plant which normally grows under arid conditions will not be happy with continued moist conditions and will ultimately die; similarly, a plant from a moist rainforest will not survive under continued aridity. Understanding these simple factors leads to more success with pot cultivation.

Terrestrials may grow as annuals, biennials or perennials.

Epiphytic Plants

Those plants which grow on the surface of another plant, on rocks or other surfaces which provide support, are known as epiphytes. These plants affix themselves to the surface by means of their roots, but they do not live as parasites, that is, they do not obtain their food supply from the host plant. In the case of parasitic plants, although they appear to be attached to the surface in the manner of an epiphyte, the roots penetrate the tissues of the host plant from which they obtain their food; these species are not suitable subjects for pot cultivation.

Epiphytes include a number of different plants such as orchids, ferns such as Hare's Foot Fern, Bird's Nest Fern, Staghorn and Elkhorn, mosses, lichens and many others. This type of plant reaches its maximum development in humid rainforests with high rainfall where it is assured of a plentiful supply of moisture.

The flowering types, such as orchids, usually grow on trees and rocks in positions where they receive ample light. Whatever form of container is used when cultivating epiphytic plants, it is essential that the roots have a free flow of air. Growing epiphytes as terrestrials, i.e. in soil, is a common cause of poor results with this type of plant.

Epiphytes, with few exceptions, are perennials.

Aquatic Plants

There are a number of plants which grow entirely in water and are known as aquatic plants. Some types float on the surface, such as the water fern, *Azolla*. Others grow completely submerged, while some types, such as water lilies, may have their roots in soil beneath the water and the foliage on or above the surface of the water. A number of arid-region plants, such as Nardoo, grow in temporary water following continued rain and die down when the water dries up.

The majority of aquatic plants cannot be grown successfully out of water, but species such as Nardoo can be grown as terrestrials provided adequate water is provided.

The majority of aquatic plants are perennials.

Forms of Plant Growth

Under natural conditions of plant growth, various features, such as the length of time the plant lives and the nature and form of its growth, allow plants to be conveniently arranged into the following groups.

Annuals

The term "annual" is given to those plants which last for only one year, that is, they germinate from seed, grow, flower, produce fruit (i.e. seed) and die in the one year.

Biennials

As the name suggests, biennials are plants which last for two years, germinating from seed and usually producing only leaves and storing food in their first year, flowering and fruiting in the second year and then dying.

Perennials

Those plants which grow for a number of years are known as perennials.

Herbs

A herb is a plant with soft stems and branches which do not become woody, unlike shrubs and trees. Herbaceous plants may be annuals, biennials or perennials.

Shrubs

The term "shrub" is applied to lower growing, woody stemmed perennials, usually with several stems arising at or near ground level; they may grow in an erect, bushy manner, or the stems may be prostrate against the ground, or spreading to procumbent. Larger shrubs may adopt the habit of small trees.

Trees

Trees may be regarded as plants which develop a main stem or trunk, usually more than three metres in height and commonly without branches on the lower part, but with a head of branches and leaves. Smaller trees may adopt the habit of shrubs, there frequently being no clear line between a tree and a larger shrub.

Climbers, Creepers, Vines

The terms "climber", "creeper" or "vine" may be applied to those plants whose stem, unless supported, is not stiff enough to grow in an upright manner. Many of these plants provide the necessary support by special twining outgrowths known as tendrils; in others, the stem or leaf stalk may twine around some adjacent object, while others may form aerial roots which grow on to an adjoining object. Some plants grow with their stems in close contact with the ground and may form a mat-like growth.

Livistona species and *Cordyline* growing in container against the wall of a building in full shade.

2. Growth Characteristics

Nature of Leaves and Stems

Plants produce stems and leaves according to their requirements. In younger, vigorous specimens, numerous new leaves and stems are formed. As the plant becomes older and more balanced, the rate of growth slows down and the production of new shoots and leaves is much reduced, which may result in the plant becoming less attractive. One of the objects of pruning a mature plant is to alter its growth balance, by encouraging it to produce new shoots and leaves in a manner similar to that of young plants and so restore a more attractive appearance. If this balance is altered too severely, by too-heavy pruning, the plant may die.

New growth is greatly influenced by the amount of light, variations in temperature and the availability of moisture and nutrients; an excess of any of these can have a damaging effect on different forms of plants.

Much better results may be obtained when cultivating a particular plant if the natural habitat under which it grows is known; for example, a species which normally grows in moist shaded conditions may be damaged when grown in a hot, sunny position.

One of the advantages of pot cultivation is that a potted plant may be moved into different situations until one which suits the particular plant is found.

Nature of Roots

Plants vary considerably in the type and number of roots they develop. The number and vigour of roots formed, which correspond in general to the activity of leaves and new growth, are greatly influenced by the nature of the soil, that is, by texture and drainage, availability of moisture, warmth, nutrients, the presence of disease-producing organisms and other factors.

An illustration of how roots move towards moisture is readily seen in plants potted in too-heavy soil or too large a pot, when the roots grow to the sides and bottom of the pot where the water passes more freely. By providing a well drained soil which allows water to pass through freely, a much better root growth will develop within the soil in the pot. When plants are watered lightly and frequently, the roots grow towards the upper surface, where they are much more subject to damage by heat and drying out. Any watering programme should be aimed at encouraging deep root growth.

As more plants are lost as a result of problems with the roots from from any other cause, it is important when selecting a plant for cultivation that one with a vigorous root growth is chosen. When the plant is growing in a pot, it may be knocked out and the vigour of the root growth observed. Many more losses can be attributed to a plant having a poorly developed initial root system rather than to poor cultivation.

In bonsai plant culture, the practice is to develop a strong root system from early stages by cutting the stronger roots back to stimulate the growth of the weaker ones; this practice is continued throughout the life of the plant. It must always be remembered that when any roots are cut the upper growth of the plant should be cut back accordingly.

Nature of Flowering

Flowering plants fall into two chief groups:

1. Long-day plants which flower in late spring and summer.
2. Short-day plants which flower in late autumn and winter.

Between the two are a number of intermediate forms which flower at various times.

As flower buds in woody-type plants, such as trees and shrubs, may take up to twelve months to develop, it is important that the plant should be provided with maximum light from one flowering period to the next. Moving a free-flowering plant into a shaded position for an extended period may reduce or prevent flowering.

The time taken from seed to flowering stage in different types of plants varies considerably. While in annuals flowering may take only a few weeks, in shrubs, trees, bulbs and orchids the time may vary from one to ten years before the first flowers are produced. To overcome this long waiting period, use is frequently made of plants propagated from cuttings and offsets taken from a mature flowering specimen.

Growth Period

All plants, whether evergreen or deciduous, have definite periods of maximum growth and resting periods. The number of hours of light and variations in temperature, coupled with adequate moisture, are the main governing factors in plant growth. Growth reaches its maximum in the long hours of summer and the minimum occurs in the shorter hours of winter. Even in periods of maximum growth there are short resting times, when the rate of growth slows down as the new shoots and leaves are strengthened by the deposition of plant tissue.

It is important to understand growth factors, because endeavouring to stimulate a plant into growth by overwatering and use of fertilisers frequently results in losses.

Vegetative growth, that is, the production of new shoots and leaves, can be stimulated artificially by providing increased hours of light and higher temperature for several weeks where necessary.

Light Requirements

Plants require various amounts of light, depending upon the habitat where they normally grow. Generally those plants which come from shaded habitats have softer, darker green leaves due to the more moist conditions and the greater amount of chlorophyll which is needed in the leaves for the purpose of photosynthesis in the lesser light available. Plants growing in full sunlight usually have some protective covering against the intense light and heat, and the leaves may be small, hard and tough and hang in a vertical manner to reduce evaporation, as in eucalypts.

Most of the very floriferous species of plants grow in positions where they receive maximum sunlight at some part of the day; when these plants are placed in shaded positions, flowering may not occur or is reduced.

It is essential to remember that plants require an adequate amount of light in order to be able to carry out the process of photosynthesis, which process provides the greater part of the plant's requirements.

Many failures of plants to flower when grown indoors are due to inadequate light; this is one of the reasons why so many foliage-type plants are grown indoors rather than floriferous species. Although some species of plants which naturally grow in low light conditions are able to cope with lesser light indoors, inadequate light may ultimately result in their death.

Where artificial lighting is used to provide light, the requisite amount of light for photosynthesis may be provided by a standard 100 watt incandescent light globe fixed 90 cm from the leaves. One problem with using this form of light is the heat created by the globe. An alternative is to use a fluorescent light tube fixed 22 to 30 cm above the plant. The artificial light period should not exceed sixteen hours per day.

3. Containers

An almost unlimited number of plant containers is available today. Made from a great range of materials, from simple, thin, plastic pots to artistic vessels of glazed ceramic ware, there is one to suit almost every type of plant and situation. Each type of container has its particular use and appeal.

The modern trend is to grow potted specimens in plastic containers and to place plant and plastic pot inside decorative ceramic pots or cane baskets for display purposes. This method gives flexibility, allowing different plants, particularly those in full flower, to be brought indoors in succession, even if only for short periods, without going to the expense of purchasing large numers of decorative pots. With indoor foliage plants, where one can afford the space to keep several plants outdoors "resting", moving the plants from indoors to outdoors results in much fresher looking specimens, as most plants show stress after extended indoor cultivation unless ideal conditions for growth are available.

Points in Selecting a Container

1. The sides of the pot should preferably taper only slightly towards the bottom, as this permits a wider soil zone in the root area and helps with drainage.
2. Except for special display containers without drainage holes, all containers should have provision for water to escape easily.
3. The depth of the pot should not exceed the width, preferably being two-thirds of the width. Where the depth is greater than the width, additional drainage material should be placed in the bottom of the container.
4. Containers with only one hole in the bottom, as found in most terracotta pots, should have two or three additional holes drilled in the bottom. If extra holes are not possible, extra care must be taken during potting to ensure that the single hole is not blocked.
5. Plastic containers with holes at the bottom edges of the pot should be checked to ensure that the holes were not blocked during manufacturing. Any obstructing material should be removed.
6. The type of container eventually chosen will depend on one's personal requirements, likes and dislikes.

Advantages and Disadvantages of Different Types of Containers

Plastic Containers

1. Plastic containers have the advantage of being light and flexible. They are obtainable in a wide variety of different shapes and colours. Most are made with only a slight taper, thus providing more space for roots and aiding drainage.

A range of different plastic containers.

2. Drainage holes in plastic containers are more effective than in other types of materials, as several holes are usually formed at the bottom edge, slightly under the pot. Extra holes are easily made.
3. As plastic material is impervious, evaporation does not occur through the container, thus reducing watering, particularly when the plant is to grow in direct sunlight.
4. All plastic materials are affected by direct sunlight, which eventually causes the pots to become brittle and crack. The rate of deterioration depends upon the thickness and quality of the plastic used in the manufacture and the amount of direct sunlight received. Plastic containers kept in the shade can have a long life.
5. In dry areas the multiple holes around the edge of the pot may result in more rapid drying of the soil in the pot, unless protected, for example, by surrounding the lower part of the container with a layer of gravel.

A plant of *Orthrosanthus multiflorus* in a 20 cm plastic container in which it has been growing for 3 years.

A plant of *Eleaocarpus reticulatus* (pink form about 1.2 m high) in a 20 cm plastic container in which it has been growing for 3 years.

A plant of *Araucaria heterophylla* about 2 m high in a 30 cm plastic container, repotted about 2 years ago, growing outdoors but brought indoors to use as a Christmas tree.

Ceramic Containers

Unglazed Terracotta 1. Terracotta pots often have a more aesthetically pleasing appearance than those made from plastic or cement.
2. The sides of terracotta pots are distinctly tapered to the bottom, which has the disadvantage of reducing the root space and restricting drainage.
3. Pots are usually manufactured with only one hole in the bottom, which may be an advantage in dry areas, but it does reduce drainage; this can be overcome by drilling additional holes in the bottom and taking care to ensure that holes are not blocked by potting material.
4. Evaporation through the sides of the container may result in an encrustation of white salts on the surface. In shady positions the moist surface of the pot may favour the growth of algae and mosses. Evaporation through the pot results in the need for more frequent watering, particularly in hot, dry, exposed positions.
5. Large pots are heavy, making them more difficult to move about.
6. Pots must be handled carefully to prevent breakage.

Glazed Terracotta 1. This form of pot is attractive and decorative, particularly for indoor use as dress containers for plants in plastic pots.
2. The glazed surface overcomes the problem of evaporation.
3. Drainage, weight and liability to damage is similar to unglazed pots.

Cane baskets and small ceramic hanging pots.

A selection of large glazed ceramic pots from Malaysia.

An array of glazed Chinese pots and bonsai trays.

Large glazed ceramic pots from China.

Cane baskets and modern glazed pots.

A group of contemporary coloured glazed pots.

A group of large earthenware pots and trays.

A group of modern glazed pots.

A group of glazed Chinese pots.

Large glazed pots from Thailand.

Cement Containers

1. Cement containers make attractive large tubs, as they can be moulded to various shapes with various surface patterns. The surface may also be painted with a flat paint to suit a particular colour scheme.
2. This form of pot or tub is usually very heavy, making it more difficult to move around. They require careful handling to prevent breakage.
3. Drainage may be a problem unless several drainage holes are provided.
4. The inner surface of new containers should be treated with an alum solution to neutralise free alkaline substances from the cement.

Planter Troughs and Boxes

Plastic Those manufactured from expanded polystyrene plastic substances are light and most useful for indoor uses in positions not exposed to direct sunlight. They deteriorate rapidly in direct sunlight.

Wooden 1. Unless these troughs are manufactured from rot-resistant timbers such as western red cedar or chemically treated pine, the timber soon rots.
2. Joints between timber allow water to escape; for indoor use, the container must be lined with plastic sheeting with the corners turned inwards not cut.

Baskets

Wire Baskets 1. Baskets made from galvanised wire are still popular for growing plants.
2. Linings for baskets are of various types, including bark from paperbark trees, coconut fibre, palm fibre and in more recent times thin sheets of material similar to that used for domestic insulation, such as rockwool batts.
3. Linings tend to break down due to rot, as they are in constant contact with moist soil.
4. As baskets dry out very rapidly, more frequent watering is required.

Wooden Baskets 1. Wooden baskets are often made in interesting shapes. They are ideal for some types of plants such as spillover forms and orchids.
2. Where plants which require soil are to be grown, coarse material such as large pieces of charcoal, may be packed along the spaces between timbers as soil is placed in position, or linings similar to wire baskets may be used.
3. The timber used in the basket must be rot resistant, such as Western Red Cedar or pressure-treated pine. Wire for jointing the timber should be copper to prevent rusting, or else nylon cord may be used.
4. As with wire baskets, frequent and heavy watering is required.

Plastic covered wire hooks, wire baskets and plastic planter trays.

Various sized, specially made, rockwool type liners for wire baskets.

Material for Growing Epiphytic Plants

1. Thick pieces of sheet cork (not reconstituted cork) are most satisfactory for growing small orchids, as they are light and do not rot.
2. Slabs of *Dicksonia* tree fern make satisfactory bases on which to grow orchids and other plants.
3. Well-weathered sound pieces of hardwood are very satisfactory on which to grow orchids and other plants.
4. Pieces of branch from paperbark trees (*Melaleuca*) are satisfactory for growing orchids and other plants.

Supports for Hanging Pots and Baskets

Various types of supports may be used for attaching hanging baskets and pots. It is important that these be strong enough to carry the necessary weight. Where pot-hooks or nails are used, it is important that they be of sufficient size and fixed securely enough to withstand the weight of the hanging plant.

Hangers may be made from materials varying from leather strands for small containers, artistic woven string types and chains of various forms to those fabricated from wire.

A number of simple wire hangers are shown in the illustrations. These may be fabricated from coat-hangers or wire of similar thickness. Examples of wire supports made from heavy gauge wire are shown for attaching hangers to beams. To assist in fabricating wire hangers, pieces of small diameter pipe, such as copper tube, and heavy-duty pliers will be found useful. A wire-fabricated hook and clip for supporting a pot against a wall or similar flat surface is also illustrated.

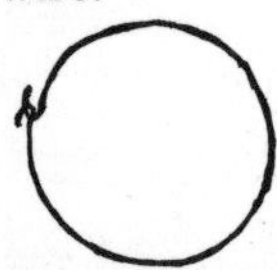

A circle of wire bent to size of pot and hooked

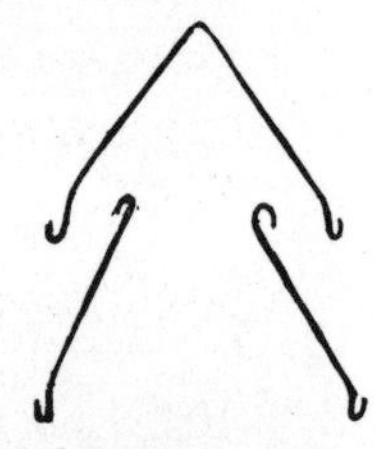

Three pieces of wire bent to attach to circle when fixed to pot

Circle of wire with hanging wires attached. Hanging wires are removed while fixing circle to pot

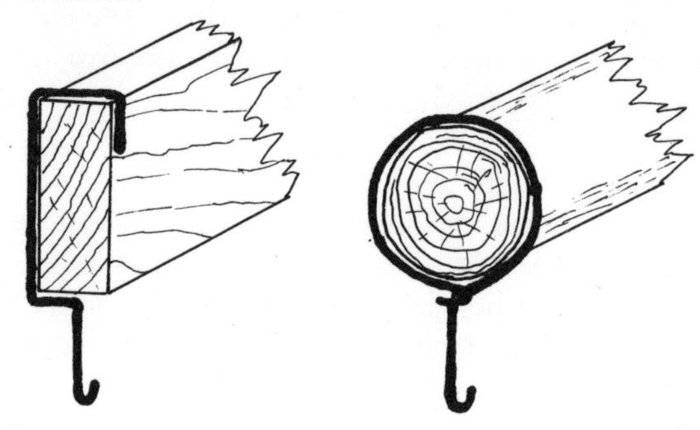

Heavy gauge wire bent to fit around a round timber beam or pipe

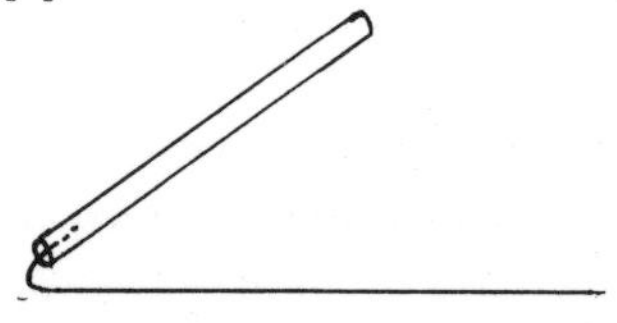

A small diameter pipe (such as a piece of copper tube) used as a simple tool for bending wire

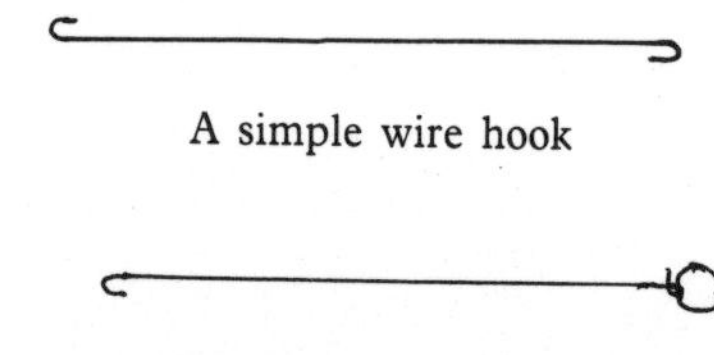

A simple wire hook

A wire hook with the upper end bent to lock around a pipe

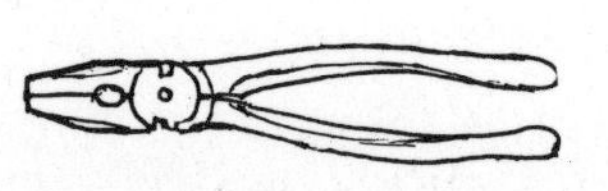

Heavy pliers for working wire

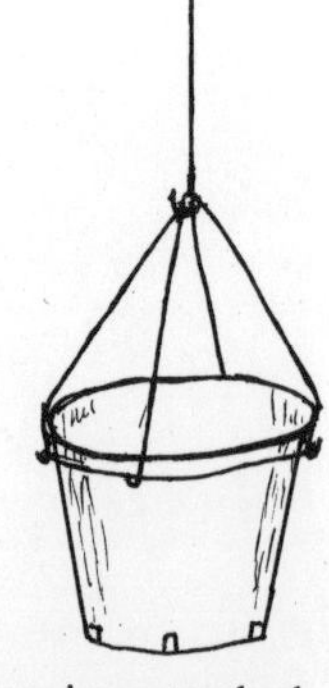

Pot with circle and hanging wires attached.

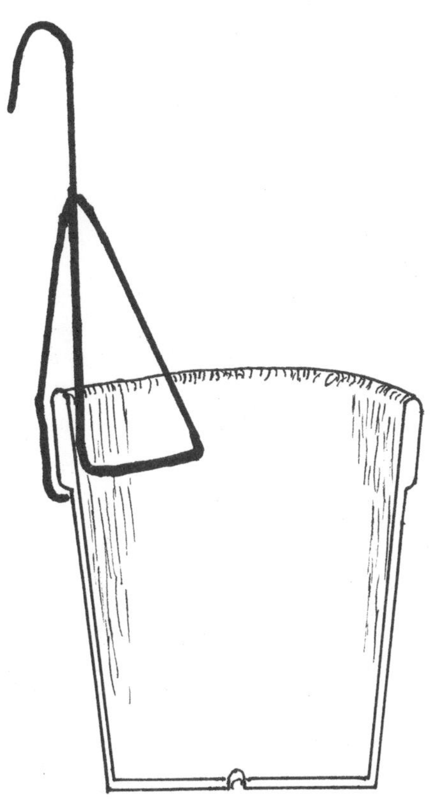

A potted orchid supported by a wire hook (shown in drawing) pushed down the side of pot.

A plant of *Hoya australis* trained on a simple wire frame made from 3 pieces of wire bent to the required shape.

A plant of *Archontophoenix cunninghamiana*, Bangalow palm, about 1 m high in a 20 cm plastic container in which it has been growing for 3 years.

4. Potting Soils

Many failures in growing plants in containers can be attributed to the use of unsuitable potting soil. Apart from use with bog and water plants which require silty type soils, potting soils which have a high clay content, fine granular structure and excessive organic content should be avoided. The fine particles in soils of this type compact together, preventing free movement of water with subsequent poor drainage. Many prepared potting soils are unsuitable for long-term pot cultivation, usually requiring the addition of coarse material.

The following basic points should be kept in mind for potting soils:

1. The soil should be light and friable, should not cake when wet or dry and should permit free movement of water at all times.
2. There should be sufficient humus (i.e. peat, compost, decayed vegetable material and the like) to hold moisture and encourage free root growth.
3. The soil should contain a percentage of loam (such as sandy bush loam or good garden loam) to provide basic plant foods.
4. There should be adequate coarse material to ensure free movement of water and drainage.
5. A simple test for the suitability of a prepared potting soil is to squeeze a handful tightly together; when released and touched it should break up freely.
6. If in doubt as to whether a particular soil mix will drain poorly, do not hesitate to add more coarse material such as river sand. A simple test is to fill a pot with the soil, apply water and see if it passes freely through the soil.

Materials for Potting Soils

Coarse Materials

River Sand River sand is usually dredged from the bed of a river and is commonly used for making concrete.

In selecting the type of river sand, give preference to sharp, coarse, granular, quartz-type material, with a minimum of fine grains or included clay. The sand may be washed to improve it. A simple way to wash sand is to fill a 9-litre (2-gallon) bucket with sand and insert a hose to the bottom of the bucket. Turn the water on slowly and, holding the hose, allow the water to bubble up through the sand, bringing with it the fine material and clay. Continue the washing until the water becomes clear.

Builders' Sand The various types of sand used by builders for brickwork should be avoided as the sand grains are fine and rounded and pack tightly together.

Other Coarse Material Washed and graded, crushed sandstone, decomposed granite and other forms of grit and gravel, excluding limestone, are all satisfactory mediums for aiding drainage in a potting mix. A naturally occurring volcanic glass known as "perlite" and specially moulded beads of foamed plastic are also satisfactory to use. Small granular pieces of charcoal free from fine dust may also be used to open up a soil mix.

Loam

Loam is soil composed of sand with varying quantities of clay.

Clayey Loam When the percentage of clay is high, it is known as clayey loam or sometimes as tennis court loam.

Sandy Loam Where the percentage of sand is high, the loam is called sandy loam or sometimes bush loam. Sandy loam should be used in preference to clayey loam.

Garden Loam The term garden loam is given to good friable garden soil. In areas where the soil is of a sandy nature, it is much lighter than where clayey or volcanic. Varying proportions of loam should be added to potting soil.

Bush Loam In sandstone areas the breakdown of the sandstone and decomposition of organic matter forms a light soil. Many types of small plants grow naturally in this type of soil which is excellent for adding to potting soils.

Potting materials left to right: **Front:** River sand, peat, bush sand. **Middle:** Water worn gravel. **Back:** Garden loam, pieces of polystyrene, pieces of broken tiles.

Peat or Peatmoss

There are two forms of peat, sphagnum and sedge peat.

Sphagnum Peat Sphagnum peak is formed from the breakdown over a long period of sphagnum moss; this type of peat does not occur in Australia in marketable quantities and is commonly imported, chiefly from Germany and Ireland.

Sedge Peat This peat is formed by the decomposition over a long period of naturally growing stiff grasses known as sedges which occur in swampy areas. Sedge peat is darker in colour than the sphagnum peat, occurs in limited quantities in Australia and is also imported from Canada. Although richer in nutrients, this form of peat breaks down more rapidly and is undesirable for long-term pot cultivation.

When using peat it is important that it will be well broken up, preferably through a coarse sieve, and allowed to soak in water for approximately 24 hours to allow it to become thoroughly wet.

Humus

Various forms of leaf mould, well rotted compost, and other forms of decomposed vegetable matter, which will form a friable, moisture-holding material, may be used in a similar manner to peat or in combination.

Sawdust

The use of sawdust, even when well rotted, should be avoided, as it uses up nitrogenous substances in the soil and, unless there is a constant balance of nutrients, toxic substances, harmful to plants, may be produced. Many nurserymen use sawdust as a substitute for peat, which frequently leads to problems in long-term pot cultivation.

Preparing the Soil

The proportion of various materials for potting soils will vary with the type of plant being grown; for example, small plants, such as *Boronia*, which naturally grow in low-nutrient soils, require less humus or peat than plants from rainforests or ferns. Although various plants may prefer different soil mixes, better growth will be obtained and the plants will live longer if the potting medium will allow free drainage at all times, even though additional watering may be required in some cases.

Always test soil mixes to see if they allow free drainage. If water does not freely drain away, add more coarse material.

Soil Sterilisation

As many losses in plants are caused by various soil fungi which attack the roots and stems of plants, causing root rot and collar rot, it is important that soil should be sterilised. This may be done by heating the soil to 60°C for thirty minutes; small quantities can be treated in the household oven. Alternatively, the soil may be treated after the plant is potted with a solution of Terrazole, ¼ teaspoon to 4 litres (1 gallon) of water, saturating the soil and washing off the foliage. One of the new fungicides such as Fongarid may be watered on to the plant. With some of the grevillea family, however, problems and losses can arise with the use of this chemical, so soil for grevilleas should preferably be heat sterilised.

Fertilisers

Mixing fertiliser with the soil should be avoided, as it may cause root damage. Where fertiliser is required, very small amounts may be added at intervals on the top of the soil, in the form of slow release pellets such as Osmocote and Nutricote; alternatively, it may be applied in liquid form by dissolving Aquasol, Zest or the like in water.

Soil Mixes

Various proportions of the materials previously discussed may be used in soil mixes. Generally, smaller growing plants, which occur naturally in low-nutrient soils, prefer a lighter type soil. When their growth is accelerated by richer soils, their lives will be shorter. Plants from rainforests and ferns require potting soils with a higher humus content and richer nature but which at the same time must be well drained. Once more try a potful of the soil mix to see if water will pass through freely. If water is retained, mix in additional course material.

In preparing soil mixes, the proportion of the various materials may vary with the nature of the substance being used, for example, a heavy, finely grained loam will require more coarse material for drainage than a more friable open type of loam. Several soil mixes are listed below as a guide, but check each for drainage and vary the proportions as necessary. Remember that light sandy mixes lacking in humus require more frequent watering.

1. A simple mixture of one part sandy bush soil and one part coarse river sand is very satisfactory for small types of plants but requires more frequent watering.
2. A mixture of one part sandy or friable garden loam, one part peat and two to three parts of coarse river sand is satisfactory for general use.
3. For ferns and rainforest type plants, a mixture of one part peat, one part leaf mould or humus, one part sandy or friable garden loam, two parts coarse river sand and one part charcoal, polystyrene pellets or perlite is satisfactory.
4. With species of plants which naturally grow in alkaline soils, two teaspoons to one tablespoon of ground limestone may be added to a 9-litre (2-gallon) bucket of potting mix.

Drainage Material

Materials to be used at the bottom of containers for drainage purposes should be of a nature that will not break down when subjected to continued moisture. Pieces of terracotta tiles, terracotta pots and coarse blue-metal are very suitable for use as drainage material. Foamed plastic polyurethane, commonly used for packaging various items such as electrical and radio equipment, is also excellent for drainage material as it is easily broken into pieces about 2 to 3 cm across and is very useful in large containers, as it reduces the weight of the potted plants.

5. Selecting and Potting

Selecting the Plant

When selecting plants avoid those which are obviously diseased; also those with numerous soft fleshy shoots which have been forced on by the free application of fertilisers, as they are more prone to disease. Such plants frequently stop their rapid growth when the source of fertiliser is removed, may languish and ultimately die.

Select a plant with a maximum number of branches which will form the basis for a bushy plant as it develops. Choose a plant in a smaller container unless an instant display plant is required or a plant for a limited period of use indoors.

Smaller Advanced Plants

In selecting plants for long-term pot cultivation, except for species of cycads, palms, cordylines, orchids and ferns, it is best to choose a small specimen. Small plants allow the specimen to be trained to one's particular requirements and maximum root growth can be encouraged from an early stage. By growing plants in smaller containers and gradually repotting into larger pots over an extended period, the growth of a plant can be regulated.

However, an advanced flowering plant is hard to resist and can be used to provide an instant display, even if its life will only be short. Generally, advanced plants are unsatisfactory for long-term pot cultivation and are usually difficult to keep to necessary requirements.

Plants Grown from Seed or Cuttings

In selecting shrubs it is best to try and obtain those which have been propagated from cuttings, rather than those raised from seed, as seedlings may take some years to reach flowering stage. Plants which have been propagated from cuttings taken from mature plants will flower at a much earlier stage, even within twelve months with faster growing types.

Some plants such as eucalypts, cycads and palms must be raised from seed as propagation from cuttings cannot be carried out successfully. Cycads and palms, particularly the former, are very slow in early growth. Palms may take several years to develop the adult leaves. Although cycads are slow in growth, the small plants make excellent potted specimens. Frequently it is possible to purchase cycad plants which have been transplanted from the wild; providing these plants are well established, they make attractive specimen plants. In selecting plants of *Cordyline*, a plant which has leaves attached to the lower part of the stem should be chosen, as once these leaves have fallen off the plants do not make new leaves from this part of the stem.

Handling the Newly Purchased Plant

Hardening the Plant

When a new plant has been purchased it should always be borne in mind that the plant will have been grown under nursery conditions, where it receives protection and conditions to maximise growth. Such plants may be soft and when taken indoors, or placed in an exposed position, frequently suffer damage to foliage and new growth. Unless it is shown that the newly purchased plant has been grown under hard conditions, it is important that it should be carefully hardened to the conditions under which it is to grow. Hardening of a plant may take two to three weeks. During the hardening period watering should not be neglected with intervals between watering being slowly increased. When watering is carried out, the soil should be thoroughly saturated. At first the plant should be placed in a protected position and then slowly moved to similar conditions under which it is to grow.

When to Repot

After a newly purchased plant has been hardened, it is ready for repotting into the particular container in which it is to grow. For potting requirements see page 00.

Potting

Potting is best carried out during spring when growth is active. This enables the plant to become re-established and develop new root growth before it is required to find additional moisture during the hotter period of summer. Potting should be avoided during winter months when growth is not active as damage to roots during repotting may result in root rot.

Before commencing potting ensure that you have at hand the required containers, soil, water and equipment such as a trowel and secateurs, as potting should be carried out without interruption. Select a protected position in which to work to avoid drying-out of roots.

Soaking

Before starting to repot, place the container with the plant to be repotted in a bucket or tub of water for about an hour to ensure that the plant absorbs enough water to prevent foliage drooping during the potting process. Where the plant is in a large heavy container, the drainage holes may be blocked temporarily and water added to the soil until it is saturated. After soaking, remove the plant from the water (or unlock the drainage holes) and allow it to drain for approximately an hour to allow soil to become firm.

Immersing pot in water until soil is saturated

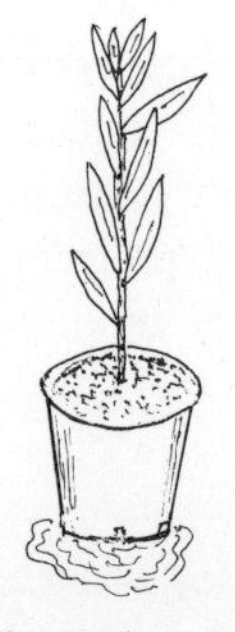

Plant draining after being removed from water

Pots showing approximate increase in size for next container when repotting.

Stages in Potting

1. Select the required container, check the drainage holes, then place a layer of coarse drainage material in the base: about 1 or 2 cm deep for small pots and 5 cm for large containers. Take care the drainage holes are not blocked during the process.

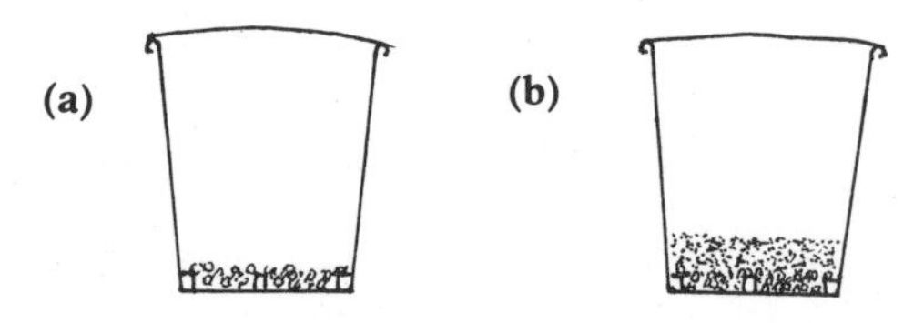

(a) After checking drainage holes, prepare slightly larger pot by placing draining material in bottom
(b) Sufficient potting soil placed in pot to bring plant to correct height

2. Place sufficient potting soil on top of the drainage material so that when the plant being potted is placed in the new container it will be at the same level as in the previous pot. Make provision for a layer of gravel to be placed on top of the soil with additional space at the top for watering.
3. After soaking and draining the plant, knock it from the pot, supporting both plant and soil with one hand. Should the plant not come out of the pot

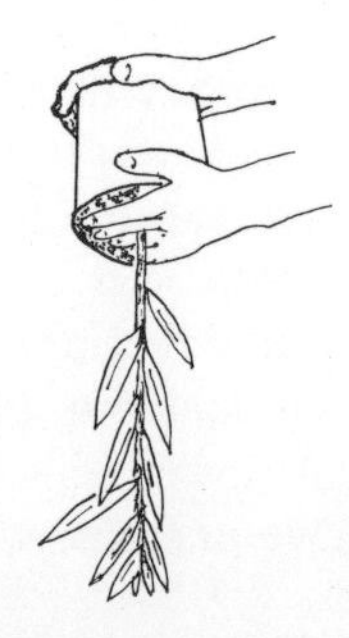

Removing plant from pot, tapping pot on a firm surface if necessary

freely, a knife or similar implement should be pushed between the soil and the pot, cutting around the pot to loosen roots which may be attached to the container. Where the roots have grown through the drainage holes and become thickened, it may be necessary to cut the pot away to release the roots and prevent damage.

4. After removing the plant from the container inspect the roots:

(a) Remove any pieces of drainage material which may have become tangled in the roots. Where there is a clump of soil in the middle of the roots, surrounded by outer roots, it should be carefully removed and the roots pushed inwards. Take care not to disturb the roots unduly as the plant may be lost.

Surface roots of plant gently loosened

(b) Where the roots are closely matted on the surface, the outer ones should be gently loosened, which is usually all that is required. Should you decide to cut off some of the roots, exercise great caution and remember to also remove an equivalent number of branchlets. Do not be over enthusiastic with your surgery, otherwise the patient may die.

(c) If the plant is small and only a few roots have developed, carefully replace it in the original pot, checking that drainage and soil remain satisfactory.

(d) Should the plant be large and of a woody nature with a poor root system, it is often better to discard it at this stage. Such a specimen tends to remain an ailing subject, finally dying.

5. Water the soil in the container and then place the plant in the new container. With one hand hold it to the required level and fill the space between the plant and the container with prepared potting soil. Gently firm the soil with the hand, taking care not to pack the potting mix too tightly, as this can lead to drainage problems.

6. After potting, water the plant well and add additional soil if necessary. Next place a layer of gravel on the surface of the soil (preferably waterworn for

Plant in pot; space around plant filled with soil and watered; layer of gravel placed on surface

appearance) to keep roots cool and assist with watering.

7. Where there has been considerable disturbance of the roots, immerse the container and plant into a bucket or tub of water and allow to soak for at least one hour.

8. Place the newly potted plant in a protected position for about a week, ensuring that watering is not neglected.

9. Place the plant in its required position. Over the next two weeks the frequency of watering should gradually be reduced to the plant's normal growth requirements.

Repotting a large *Rhododendron lochae*

Plant to be repotted.

Plant removed from pot and surface roots loosened.

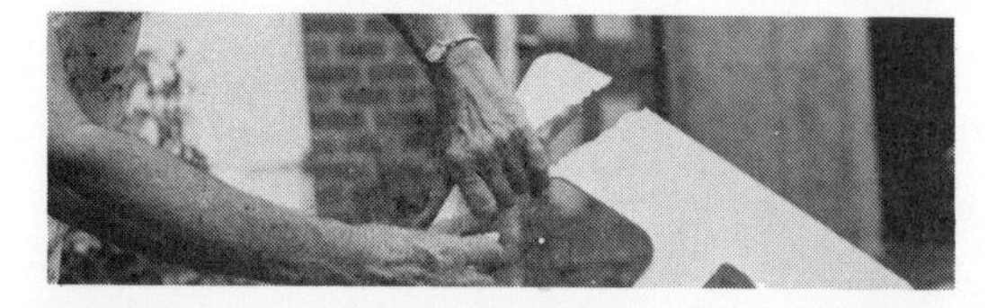

Breaking up a polystyrene packing box to provide drainage material.

Pot with a layer of polystyrene drainage material.

Plant in position in pot.

Potting complete with a layer of gravel placed on the surface of the soil and pot watered well.

Pterostylis curta, Greenhood, growing in a 12 cm pot and left in a shaded protected position.

Placing pieces of polystyrene in the bottom of a plastic container.

Container with a layer of potting soil placed over drainage material ready to receive plant.

Space between pot and plant filled with potting soil and firmed with hands.

Selecting Garden Position

Much better results will be obtained in the cultivation of plants in containers if the position in which they are to grow is suitable for the particular type of plant. A study should be made of the areas available for pot plants, taking note of the amount of, or lack of, sunlight received. Remember that a position which receives adequate sunlight during summer may be in complete shade in winter. Having determined the amount of sunlight available in the position selected, choose the type of plant which will be suitable for the conditions available.

Advantage should be taken of walls, fences and other structures which may give protection, providing that they do not interfere with the necessary sunlight. An open type decorative screen or fence may be provided if necessary. A simple bush-house makes cultivation of ferns and orchids easier.

Plants which are to be grown in suspended containers, such as baskets, should be given protection from drying winds where possible, as the free circulation of air around the plant and container brings about more rapid drying of the soil.

6. Plant Control and Pruning

Natural Growth

Young plants naturally grow rapidly with the maximum number of leaves, growing to maturity and ultimately flowering. As the plant approaches its maximum size, the rate of growth tends to slow down to the particular plant's requirements.

More than One Plant in a Container

Two or three plants may be planted in the same container when a more busy form of growth for foliage plants is required, or a more rapid spillover effect with hanging plants or more massed display of flowers is desired, particularly when smaller plants are being used. In selecting a container it may be necessary to use a larger size than for a single plant, as additional space may be required. Prepare the container as previously described on page 00. Each of the plants should be prepared for potting as described there, and the container filled with the required amount of soil as for a single plant. The selected plants are placed close together in the container with only a small space between them; and potting is carried out in the same manner as for an individual plant.

Where several plants are in the same container, more frequent watering may be required than with a single plant. Slightly more frequent application of fertiliser may be required where several plants are in the same container, but be careful here—over-fertilising may result in the loss of the plants.

Staking Plants

The staking of plants should be avoided, except for supporting creepers and providing temporary support for slender-stemmed, newly potted plants. Where the stem is supported constantly, the stem grows less sturdy and lateral root growth is reduced. By encouraging the growth of side shoots and controlling upper growth, the plant becomes balanced and self supporting. Where a temporary stake is used, it should be a small space away from the stem and the tie used between the stake and plant should allow the plant to move freely and so encourage lateral root growth. The stake should be removed as soon as possible.

Growth in Containers

The rate of growth of a plant in a container is governed by factors such as the amount and nature of soil and the nutrients it contains, the availability of moisture and adequate supply of light and temperature. These factors, as well as controlling rate of growth, may determine the ultimate size of the plant.

An example of variation in growth rates may be shown with a plant repotted from a small container into a large pot with well drained soil. The plant roots seek out the additional nutrients and moisture, resulting at first in rapid growth of the plant and then a slowing down of the rate of growth, as roots are no longer able to expand. If the repotting process is repeated too quickly, the plant grows rapidly to maturity, making it more difficult to control the size of the plant and defeating the object of long-term pot cultivation and, in many cases, reducing the length of life of the plant. In a similar manner, when plants are freely fertilised, even in small containers, rapid growth results, making it more difficult to control the plant and frequently reducing the life of the plant.

Except for annuals and short-lived perennials, the object of pot cultivation should be to develop a strong healthy plant which will live for a long time without requiring unnecessary attention.

Root Growth

Small Plants in Large Containers

When a small plant is grown in a large container, even with well drained soil, the roots grow away from

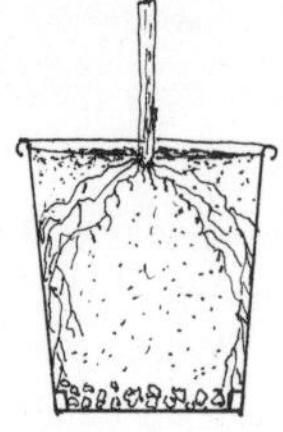

Roots growing away from centre of pot in heavy soil or too large a pot

the central part of the soil to the outer edges against the sides of the pot, where there is better aeration and drainage. Even with well drained soil, the middle of the container may become soggy with the plant producing few roots as conditions are conducive to root rot, and thus unsatisfactory for cultivation.

Plants in Small Containers

When small plants are grown in small containers with well drained soil, the roots, as well as growing towards the edges of the soil, grow downwards through the smaller soil mass as drainage can occur more freely. This form of root growth results in a maximum number of roots developing from an early

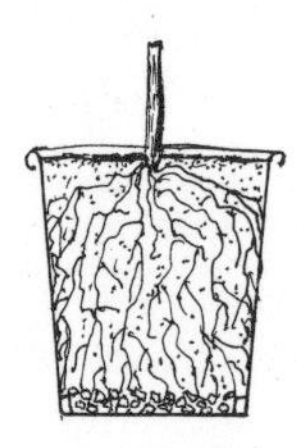

A well grown plant with roots well developed throughout soil

stage, with plant growth reducing the possibility of root rot. It is thus important that plants should be started in small containers to produce the maximum number of roots; when repotting is carried out, the next sized container to that in which the plant is growing should be used.

A good example of the effectiveness of a maximum number of roots in a soil mass may be found with bonsai plant cultivation. In these plants the aim is to produce a large number of roots in relation to the small soil mass and the resultant potted specimen lives for many years.

Plant Training

To help keep potted plants looking at their best, the development of the plant should be controlled from the early stages to increase the number of branches and maximum amount of foliage. It is a mistake to allow a potted specimen to grow to a large plant and then carry out severe pruning to endeavour to bring the plant back under control. Severe pruning, particularly of older stems, frequently results in the loss of the plant.

Tip Pruning

Tip pruning, removing the soft growing tips of the branchlets, may be simply carried out by pinching out the tips with the thumb and finger. This form of

Tip pruning a small Mint bush with fingers.

pruning is used to help shape the plant and make it more busy as additional shoots develop from the base of the leaves. In removing the growing tips it is important not to continually remove the tips of the shoots as they develop, as it may prevent the plant from growing. The shoots should be allowed to grow to a length to suit requirements, at which stage the tip is removed. As additional shoots develop, they should be allowed to grow to the required length before removing the tip. With regular attention a plant may be shaped to personal requirements.

Plant Shaping

As an added interest potted plants may be developed in a fan or espalier manner by providing a frame of light timber or heavy gauged wire in a particular shape, for example, triangular, square or oval. The frame is supported by two legs nailed to or wired to the frame. The legs are pushed deeply between the sides of the container and the soil. As the potted plant grows, the branches are tied back to the frame and gradually developed to the required shape, encouraging growth of small branches to form a good cover.

Various types of climbing and twining plants may easily be trained to a frame. For such plants a large globular wire-shaped frame may be constructed with four or more wires bent to the shape, with the ends pushed into the soil and the tops tied together where they intersect. Horizontal circular rings of wire may be attached to the shaped wires. With twining and climbing plants it is necessary to direct the new growth back on to the frame as it develops.

Clipped Plants

Suitable subjects for clipping are strong-growing plants with smaller leaves, such as tea trees and paperbarks (*Leptospermum* species and *Melaleuca* species), *Darwinia citriodora*, smaller leaved lillypillies such as *Syzygium paniculatum* and *S. luehmannii*, and *Callistemon salignus*. Clipping of the foliage should be commenced at an early stage to produce the maximum number of branchlets. During the growing season clipping should be carried out frequently to maintain a close cover of leaves, care being exercised not to cut thick branches during cutting. The new coloured foliage is most attractive and with species such as *Leptospermum petersonii* and *Darwinia citriodora*, clipping produces a delightful citron aroma.

General Pruning

The object of pruning is to encourage new growth as well as keep the plant to a desired shape. Plants which are allowed to grow without pruning adjust their growth and number of leaves to the plant's requirements, which may produce a straggly appearance. When pruning is carried out, the balance established by the plant is disturbed and the plant reacts by producing new growth. With those plants such as *Leptospermum squarrosum* which produce flowers on the old wood, flowers may not be produced when the older stems are continually removed.

1. A general rule which should be applied to pruning plants is to avoid cutting back into old hard woody stems.
2. Another general rule is that not more than one-third of the length of the previous year's growth should be removed during pruning.
3. It is important that pruning should be carried out at the correct time.

(a) Except for deciduous plants, avoid pruning when growth is dormant, as branches may die back and the plant may die.
(b) Prune immediately after flowering as most plants produce new growth following flowering.
(c) Apart from tip pruning and clipping (see pages 26–7) avoid heavy pruning during active growth. When new growth is allowed to grow to an advanced stage before pruning, much of the value of pruning is lost and flower buds may be removed.
(d) With plants which may not flower regularly, such as eucalypts, prune in spring, just as growth is about to commence.
(e) When branches are pruned, make the cut just above a side branch where possible.

7. Watering

Incorrect watering, coupled with poor drainage, may be considered the main reason for losses of potted plants. Irrespective of the type of plant being grown, it is essential that when it is watered, the soil and roots should be thoroughly saturated. Bear in mind that light frequent watering induces the roots to grow

Frequent light watering brings root growth towards surface

towards the surface of the soil, where they are subject to drying out, often causing the loss of the plant. Frequent heavy watering, which creates boggy soil conditions, is conducive to the growth of various soil fungi, which may cause root and collar rot, and eventually plant loss.

The frequency of watering is influenced by different conditions, for example:

1. The type of plant: a plant with small hard leaves transpires less moisture from the soil than one with larger soft type foliage; likewise a small sized plant will use less water than one which is larger.
2. The location of the potted plant is important; thus a plant growing in a hot sunny position or one which is subject to drying winds will use considerably more water than a plant growing in a shaded, protected position. Plants in suspended baskets or pots dry out more rapidly than those in containers on the ground.
3. The nature of the container is also important, for example:

(a) A lined wire basket will dry out more rapidly than a plastic basket of the same size.

(b) An unglazed terracotta pot allows water to be evaporated from the sides, whereas a plastic container, glazed terracotta or painted cement pot prevents this evaporation.

(c) Holes at the bottom of the sides of the container, as found in most plastic pots, provide good drainage, but, in dry and windy locations, unless the drainage holes are protected, the soil dries out more rapidly than in pots where the drainage holes are in the bottom of the container, as found in terracotta pots.

4. During warm weather when the plant is in active growth there is a much greater use of water than when the weather is cool and the growth is dormant.
5. When watering is carried out, add water until it begins to flow out of the drainage holes.

When to Water

For long-term cultivation of pot plants, watering should be regulated to provide the plant's minimum requirements. This can be judged by observing the plant's foliage, which will begin to droop slightly when watering is insufficient. It is important not to allow the plant to become distressed and droop badly as new growth will become dried out and leaves may die; this particularly applies to ferns. When bad drooping occurs, the container and plant should be stood in a bucket or tub of water for several hours until it recovers.

It is important to start regulating the watering two to three weeks after potting, extending the periods between waterings, and aim at producing a strong plant with firm growth rather than one with lush foliage. Weather plays an important part in the frequency of watering; a dry atmosphere dries out the plant more rapidly than does moist air.

1. With established plants in a large container, a weekly watering will usually be sufficient during spring; with a plant in a smaller container, watering may be required twice per week.
2. During cold weather watering may only be required fortnightly for larger containers and weekly for smaller containers.
3. In hot sunny positions, and particularly where you have large plants in small containers, watering

may be required more frequently, but once again observe your plant and only give additional watering if necessary.

4. Suspended plants in baskets and containers generally require more frequent watering than plants standing on the ground.

(a) During spring plants growing in lined wire baskets may require watering two to three times per week and daily during hot summer conditions. During winter weekly watering may be adequate.

(b) During spring plants in plastic type baskets and other containers may require watering weekly; during summer two to three times per week may be required and in winter weekly or fortnightly waterings may be adequate; once more, observe your plant for its watering requirements.

5. Standing the container in a bucket or trough containing 5 to 7 cm of water for about two hours weekly or fortnightly induces good deep root growth, but it does require more effort.

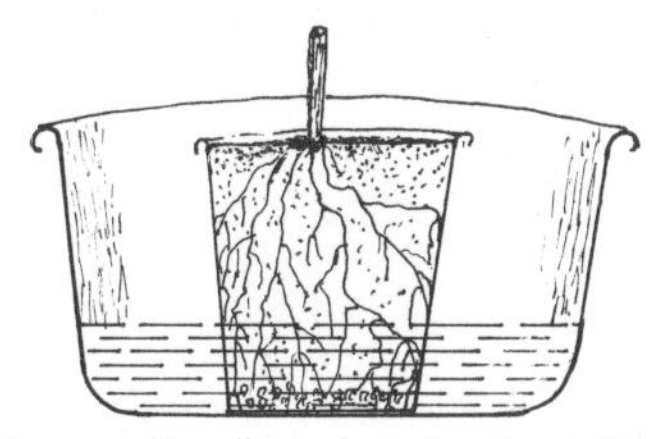

Watering plants by standing container in about 7 cm of water

Plastic pot with clip-on tray to catch water.

Plastic pot with clip-on tray removed showing attachment holes.

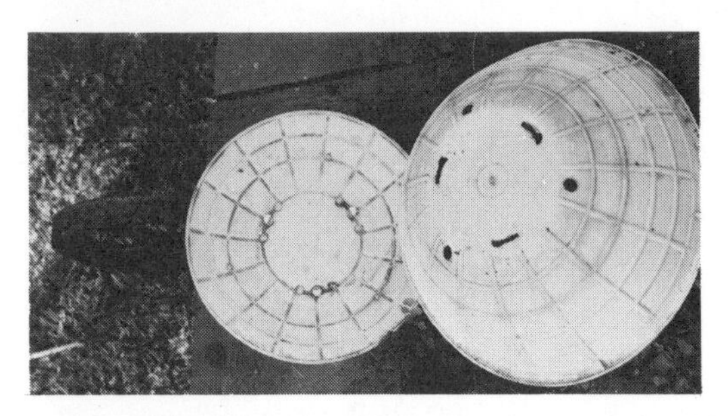

Plastic basket with the clip-on tray removed showi attachment holes.

Plastic basket with a clipped-on tray used for holding water overflow.

8. Maintenance of Container Grown Plants

Apart from watering, repotting, control of insects and fungal diseases, pruning and fertilising, potted plants require a general maintenance programme for satisfactory results.

1. Check drainage holes regularly to ensure that they do not become blocked with soil or other obstructions.
2. Roots emerging from drainage holes should be cut off as they appear.
3. Containers standing on the ground should be lifted periodically to ensure that roots are not growing into the ground. Where this occurs, the roots should be cut off and the container and plant stood in water for about 2 hours to ensure that the plant does not suffer a setback.

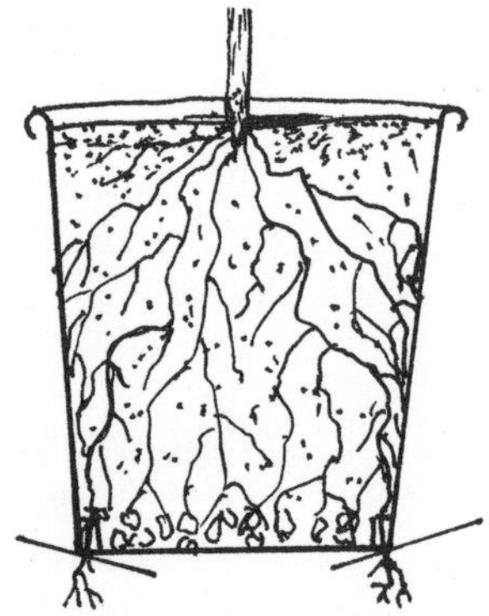

Roots growing out of drainage holes and cut off where shown

4. Soil and other debris collecting around the container should be regularly removed.
5. Where gravel is placed on the ground to facilitate drainage, it should be periodically hosed to remove deposits of fine soil.
6. In addition to removing weeds and moss growth, additional gravel or soil should be added to the container as necessary.
7. Except where the plant is growing in full sunlight, the container should be regularly turned to maintain even foliage growth.
8. The soil in the container should be treated against fungus diseases by watering with Terrazole or Fongarid (excluding *Banksia* family) at two monthly intervals during late spring and summer, at strengths recommended by the manufacturer.

Roots growing through the drainage hole of a large terracotta pot.

9. Treat the soil in the container twice a year against eelworm with a sprinkling of Nemacur.
10. Immediate attention should be given to attack of foliage by insects or fungi.
11. Control the shape of the plant by tip pruning and prune when required.
12. When the plant has been in the same container for some time it may be very lightly fertilised at three-monthly intervals during spring and summer, if so desired. If fertilisers are used with Australian natives, it is most important that they be applied sparingly.

9. Growing Annuals and Perennials

Annuals

Annuals such as the daisies *Helipterum* (sometimes known as *Acrolinium*) are not usually available as plants, and so must be raised from seed. The species *Helipterum manglesii* and *H. roseum* are usually available from seedsmen (sometimes under the name of *Acrolinium*). Seeds should be sown in February for flowering in spring.

Raising Seedlings

Fill a shallow seed tray or seedling punnet with light potting soil and consolidate it; sprinkle seed over the surface or sow it in rows, cover the seed to twice its depth with potting soil and then water well. Place the seed box in a sunny position and water daily, ensuring that the soil is not allowed to dry out. Seeds germinate in about one to two weeks. Allow the small seedlings to grow until three to four pairs of leaves have developed, when they are ready for transplanting.

Potted Seedlings

Fill a wide container, basket or planter tray with light potting soil and make several holes in the soil to provide spacing of 5 to 7 cm between plants. Water the holes. Prick out individual seedlings using a small table fork or similar implement, place a seedling in each hole and fill in the soil around the plant. Repeat the process until all plants are in position, then water well.

Growing Plants On

The potted seedlings should be kept in a sunny position and watered every few days. As seedlings are frequently attacked by aphis, the plants should be sprayed whenever an attack is noticed with a spray such as Malathion, following the manufacturer's instructions.

Perennials

Plants such as Sturt's Desert Pea (*Clianthus formosa*) must be raised from seed, which is available from specialist seed merchants. As the seed coat is very hard, the seed should be placed on a piece of garnet grit sandpaper and lightly rubbed with another piece of sandpaper held around a block of wood. The treated seed is then placed in a cup, covered with boiling water and allowed to soak and swell overnight before sowing. Seed is best sown at the end of July for flowering in early summer.

Raising Seedlings

Fill a large deep container such as a 25 cm pot with light potting soil and consolidate well. Sow two or three seeds in the soil at a depth of approximately twice the thickness of the seed and water well. Place the container in a sunny position. The seedlings should appear within a week if properly treated. These seedlings do not transplant satisfactorily and should be allowed to grow in the container where they are sown, which should be kept in full sun at all times. As the plants are prone to damping off, the soil should be watered with Captan or Fongarid when the seedlings appear. This treatment should be repeated in about a fortnight. Growth is rapid and the plant will soon trail over the sides of the container. As an alternative seeds may be sown in a deep hanging basket or pot, producing a very interesting trailing plant.

10. Propagating from Cuttings

Plants may be propagated from selected pieces of an existing plant. The time required for formation of roots varies with different types of plants. Soft herbaceous forms of plants such as *Brachycome, Isotoma, Pratia, Dampiera* and similar types, may develop roots within two to three weeks, whereas hard wooded types such as *Grevillea* may take two to six months.

It is important to choose the correct type of cuttings. The older, hard, woody parts of the stems should be avoided as roots will not develop successfully. In a similar manner, except for herbaceous types, the soft, fleshy, brittle growing shoots should also be avoided as they commonly die or take considerable time to form roots. Green, firm stems, which are flexible but not brittle, usually give best results.

Selecting and Preparing Cuttings

In most cases, the best time for taking cuttings is in spring and early autumn. Select pieces of stem about 10 cm long in which the growing tip is just beginning to expand; and avoid the stems where new growth is advanced.

After collecting the cutting, using a very sharp knife or secateurs, carefully remove the leaves on the lower half of the stem and make a cut in the lower part of the stem at a leaf joint. Next remove the growing tip. It is most important that at no time should cuttings be allowed to dry out; keep them in a plastic bag or stand them in water to which a small amount of Formula 20 has been added. They should be planted as quickly as possible.

Setting the Cuttings

Select a container about 12 cm in diameter and fill with a mixture of three parts coarse river sand and one part sieved peat. Consolidate the mix by bumping the pot on to a flat surface. Make holes in the mix around the edges of the container, with a piece of wire or small stick, at intervals of about 3 cm. Place a prepared cutting in each of the holes, gently firming the sand with the fingers. When all the cuttings are in position, water them well with water to which a few drops of Formula 20 has been added. The cuttings should then be covered with a plastic bag. First bend two pieces of wire into U-shapes and push into the sand to support the bag. Slip the bag over the wires and the pot and fasten the

A pot showing cutting set in sand and peat with wires to support a plastic bag.

Plastic bag fitted over wire frame and tied around pot with a strip of stocking.

bottom of the bag around the pot. Alternatively, using a larger bag, stand the pot inside the bag and tie the top with a twist-tie. Stand the pot in a protected, well lit position, but away from hot sun. The plastic bag should be kept under observation; while there is still moisture on the inner surface, watering is not required. In a cool protected position, watering may not be required during the rooting period. It is most important, however, to water when there is no moisture on the inside of the bag. About three months after the cuttings have been placed in position, the bag may be removed and cuttings checked for roots. This is done by watering well and then gently pulling on the cuttings. If they have rooted they will stay firmly in place; if they come away easily, roots have not developed, in which case replace the bag. The rooted cuttings and sand are knocked from the pot and separated. Each is potted into a container in a similar manner to seedlings and is then allowed to develop as a seedling.

Herbaceous Type Plants

With soft type plants, such as *Brachycome* and *Isotoma*, a small piece is planted into a container of potting soil, placed in a protected position and watered daily. Roots will develop and the plant is allowed to grow on in the same container. Plants such as violets may be cut into small sections, planted in a prepared container with potting soil and allowed to grow on.

11. House Plants

The term "house plants" is used here rather than "indoor plants" as only a small number of plants will grow successfully indoors for extended periods, unless ideal conditions for growth are provided (such as those in a glasshouse). For successful growth indoors, plants require adequate light, absence of dry air movement, sufficient humidity, and freedom from gaseous fumes, dusty conditions and hot dry temperatures, such as those found when room heaters are used. Plants grown indoors for extended periods commonly suffer from burning and drying of the edges and ends of leaves, loss of leaf colour, elongation and distortion of growth, root root and attack by various insects and fungi.

Those plants which normally grow under lower light conditions, as found in the rainforest, are generally more suitable for growing indoors than those plants which grow in full sunlight. It is possible to move any plant indoors, even if only for a day, for example, to enjoy a potted specimen in full flower. By having several potted specimens, it is possible to move a plant indoors for say two weeks and then replace it with another plant, while the plant from indoors is moved outside to a protected position to recover; this ensures a much more attractive indoor specimen. Having four plants makes it possible to give each plant two weeks indoors and six weeks outdoors in more favourable conditions for growth.

A number of factors influence the successful cultivation of indoor plants.

Type of Plant

As mentioned above, some plants will grow more successfully indoors than others. Those plants which are normal inhabitants of rainforests, with larger, often shiny, dark green leaves, are more adaptable for cultivation indoors when growing as foliage plants than those plants with small harder leaves from plants in dry heathland and woodland areas where full sunlight is received. Although there are exceptions to the rule, these characteristics should be considered when selecting plants for use indoors as foliage plants. Plants which are more readily available and adaptable for indoor use include the Silky Oak (*Grevillea robusta*); different *Ficus* species, for example *F. microcarpa* var. *hillii*, *F. benjamina*; various lillypillies such as *Syzygium crebrinervis*, *S. paniculata*, *S. leuhmannii*, *Acmena smithii*; various pittosporums, for example *P. undulatum*, *P. revolutum*; the Umbrella Tree, *Schefflera actinophylla*; *Cordylines* such as *C. stricta*, *C. rubra*; various palms, for example, the Kentia Palm, *Howea fosterana*, Cabbage Tree Palm, *Livistona australis*. The ferns include the Fishbone Fern, *Nephrolepis cordifolia*, Mother Spleenwort, *Asplenium bulbiferum* and Bird's Nest Fern, *Asplenium australasicum* (syn. *A. nidus*); among the twining plants are *Cissus antarctica* and *Hoya australis*.

Light

The amount of light a plant receives indoors is one of the chief factors controlling successful cultivation. See page 10.

The amount or intensity of natural light inside the average dwelling is influenced by many factors. As an example, assume that a window is facing north and there is no obstruction to sunlight entering the window, such as curtains, blinds, overhanging eaves, verandah or trees. In this case the only part of the room where the light intensity is equal to that outside is against the lower part of the window glass not affected by any obstruction. The light intensity decreases rapidly according to the distance from the source of light, in proportion to the square of the distance. As an example, at a distance of say 60 cm from an unobstructed window, the light intensity is only approximately one-quarter of that at the window glass; similarly, at a distance of one metre, the light intensity would be only approximately one tenth; and so on. Thus it can be seen that it can be difficult to provide the required amount of light for a plant growing indoors, particularly for flowering purposes. The problem is further added to by the presence of curtains, blinds or other obstructions. A typical example of the effects of light on flowering plants can be readily demonstrated with the exotic African Violet, which many people find difficult to get to flower in spite of the use of various types of fertilisers. These plants require a high light intensity but not direct sunlight—without it, they do not flower. The light intensity may be provided with artificial light (see page 10).

Plants from rainforests and shaded gullies, which grow under low light conditions on the forest floor in their early stages of growth, are more suitable for growing indoors as foliage plants.

Air Movement and Temperature

Plants growing outdoors experience continual changes in the surrounding air caused by air movement, which is essential for the plant's successful growth and well being. During daylight the plant uses carbon dioxide from the air to carry out its process of photosynthesis, which makes a change of air necessary. The plant is also subject to a wide range of temperature changes, sometimes from extreme heat to sudden cooling, all of which has an effect on the plant's activity. At night time condensation of the moisture in the air forms dew which can relieve stresses on the plant's foliage produced during the hours of daylight.

With plants growing indoors, there is often difficulty in ensuring proper air movement and changes in temperature. Frequently indoor plants are kept in the corner of a room where air movement is restricted and temperatures remain cool. In other cases the plant may be in a position where there is a strong flow of air which may be heated and dried by cooking or other heating appliances, having considerable effect on the plant's growth. A further problem with plants grown indoors is that, as houses are generally closed at night, air movement is further restricted and temperatures do not change as they do outdoors, thus preventing the deposition of condensation or dew on the leaves; this is another advantage of which the indoor plant is deprived.

Humidity

A considerable problem with plants growing indoors is lack of humidity at most times. This dryness of the air, combined with even minimum air movement, removes moisture from the leaves resulting in the ends and edges becoming dry, dying and turning brown. This problem can be partially relieved by spraying the foliage with a fine mist spray, but under dry conditions the frequency required may become impracticable. Another method of solving the problem is to stand the plant on a large tray filled with sand or other course material which is kept moist. The evaporation of this moisture helps to add moisture to the air around the plant and can partially assist in reducing drying of leaves. Growing several plants together on a large tray with moist sand may help with the problem. It is a mistake, however, to stand the plant in a tray of water as this leads to root rot.

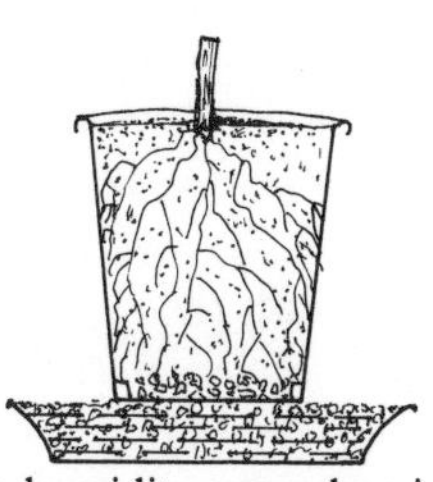

A way of providing humidity around an indoor plant: a tray filled with gravel or sand with water.

12. Bonsai

Bonsai cultivation differs completely from the cultivation of plants in standard type containers where the object is to produce a bushy, attractive foliage or flowering plant. In bonsai the object is to produce in miniature a tree or shrub displaying the features and forms of a fully-grown tree or shrub found growing naturally while cultivated in a small shallow tray. The character of the plant and its container are viewed aesthetically as one. The term "bonsai" simply means "planted in a tray". Bonsai has been practised for centuries in Japan, where these plants are regarded with veneration and handed down in families, in some cases for 200 years or more. The development of bonsai specimens requires considerable patience, care, attention and understanding, as it takes a number of years for a plant to produce a partiular form or effect. For those attempting bonsai for the first time, it is recommended that specialist books on the subject should be studied and the opportunity taken of observing established bonsai specimen plants.

There are various styles or forms of bonsai based on the characters found in plants growing in nature. For example, in a windy exposed position, such as a mountain ridge or seafront, the trunk may become bent in different directions as the tree grows; or the trunk may be short and develop a gnarled appearance; similarly, plants growing on rock shelves and cliff faces, where soil is limited and growth conditions vary with the availability of moisture, may become dwarfed, with the stem or trunk growing in a twisted or bent manner. Various names are given to these characters in bonsai: a short, straight, slightly tapered trunk is called "chokkan"; a sloping or leaning trunk "shakan"; a bent and drooping trunk "kenzai"; two trunks arising from the one base "sokan"; a tree with a stone "ishisaki", and so on. There is now a trend towards growing a number of shrubs or trees in one tray to give the appearance of a miniature forest; this is called "yoseue". There are many variations of these.

Selecting Plants

Most bonsai specimens have been developed from exotic conifers, deciduous plants and some evergreens. Only in comparatively recent years has use been made of Australian plants for bonsai purposes. As, with few exceptions, Australian plants are evergreens, they generally resent root disturbance unless handled with considerable care. This is particularly so with eucalypts.

Those who would like to try their hand at bonsai with Australian plants should commence with species such as *Ficus rubiginosa*, *Banksia serrata*, *Melaleuca alternifolia* or *Casuarina torulosa*.

Select plants which are small and particularly those showing obvious characteristics of a particular style of development.

Containers

Bonsai plants are frequently first established in a shallow standard container and a year or two later repotted into a selected bonsai pot. Bonsai pots are designed to form part of a particular bonsai arrangement and differ from standard containers generally in being shallow in relation to their width. They are of ceramic ware, glazed or unglazed, with one or more drainage holes in the bottom and often provided with short legs at the corners.

Potting Plants

Potting is best carried out in early to mid spring when growth has commenced but is not as active as in summer, because during potting roots are disturbed and cut, sometimes to enable the plant to fit the pot and to stimulate new root growth, which is essential for healthy bonsai plants. When the roots are cut, an equivalent amount of foliage must also be removed; considerable care should be exercised with both, as the shape of a plant may be altered by incorrect cutting. To prevent soil blocking the drainage holes, place a piece of vinyl mesh (as used for flyscreens) over the hole, followed by a thin layer of course river sand; next place a layer of light potting soil in the pot and position the plant; then fill the container with the potting soil, carefully consolidating with a small stick or dibbler. Water the plant well and place in a protected position for several weeks until new growth becomes evident; the plant is then moved into its selected position.

Generally, repotting is only required every two to three years or more.

Training

The development of a plant into a particular form of bonsai is a long-term process involving shaping the branches and trunk by wiring and other methods, careful pruning and constant attention. As specialised characters are aimed at in the process of developing a particular form of bonsai, it is strongly recommended that specialised books on the subject be studied as well as observing as many specimens as possible. Joining a bonsai society is also helpful.

Watering

The small amount of soil present in a bonsai pot, together with the free drainage which occurs in the shallow container, make frequent watering of this form of plant necessary, more than is required for a potted plant growing in a standard type container. As a general guide, it is most important that the pot should not be allowed to dry out before watering is carried out.

Generally, watering is required once or twice daily during summer, particularly when growth is very active. In spring and autumn, daily watering is usually necessary and in winter the intervals may be reduced. Ensure, however, that the soil does not dry out at any time.

Fertilising

Light fertilising may be carried out at three-monthly intervals during the growing season only. It is important that the plant should at no time be forced along with the use of fertiliser.

A Final Word

Do not attempt to grow bonsai plants unless you are prepared to give the constant care which is necessary. Remember that there is no fast, easy way of developing a bonsai specimen plant.

13. Growing Ferns

With few exceptions, ferns require a cool, moist, protected position, free from drying winds and protected from full sun; if this cannot be avoided, ensure that the direct rays of the sun are broken and full sun is received for very short periods only. Most ferns grow in the soil; a number of types, however, grow on the trunks of trees and rocks. They are known as epiphytes and include such ferns as Bird's Nest Ferns, Elkhorns and Hare's-Foot Ferns. Other ferns grow in water, for example, the floating fern *Azolla* and the different Nardoo *Marsilea* species. Many types of ferns under cultivation require a bush house or glass house for satisfactory results. The species discussed are confined to those which are more easily grown.

Fern Groups

1. One group of ferns has a central, single stem, usually very short, but sometimes long as in tree ferns. Although ferns in this group increase in size, they do not produce new shoots or new separate ferns from the base and cannot be divided into two or more separate plants. Within this group of ferns there are a number such as Mother Spleenwort (*Asplenium bulbiferum*), Necklace Fern (*A. flabellifolium*), Shield-fern (*Polystichum australiense*) and others which form small plants on the frond which may be removed and grown as separate plants.

2. A second group of ferns has creeping stems which may be very short as in Elkhorns (*Platycerium*), or may form large clumps as in Maidenhair Fern (*Adiantum*), Sickle Fern (*Pellaea falcata*), Fishbone Fern (*Nephrolepis cordifolia*), Rasp Fern (*Doodia aspera*) and others. There are others with widely extending creeping stems such as the Ground Fern (*Hypolepis muelleri*) which are unsuitable for pot cultivation. Among those ferns that creep on the trunks of trees and on rocks Hare's-Foot Fern (*Davallia pyxidata*), Fragrant and Kangaroo Ferns (*Microsorium scandens, M. diversifolium*), Rock Felt

Fern and Robber Fern (*Pyrrosia rupestris, P. confluens*) make suitable subjects for growing in pots and on slabs. A number of these ferns tend to grow towards the edges of the container, as with Maidenhair fern, leaving the centre of the container with dead fronds; other types, such as Hare's-Foot Fern and Kangaroo Ferns, branch freely about the soil and make attractive basket specimens which will grow for many years without repotting. If so desired, these creeping ferns may be divided into separate plants. With types such as Maidenhair Fern which grow towards the edges of the container, the older parts of the plant towards the middle of the pot may be carefully removed and the newer growth moved inwards during repotting.

Pots

Where the fern is to be repotted into a larger container, potting is carried out in a similar manner to that described on page 00, using potting soil with a high humus content.When Tree Ferns are grown in a container, a large container is required and the fern must always be kept in a shaded position.

With small divided sections of fern, a layer of soil of sufficient depth to bring the plant to the required height, is placed over the drainage material. The soil is watered well and the section of fern to be potted is placed into position. The roots are then well covered with soil, which is gently firmed, and the plant is watered well.

Ferns such as Bird's Nest or small Elkhorns may be potted into a terracotta pot slightly larger than the fern, using peat in lieu of soil.

Creeping Types

Baskets

Ferns such as Hare's-Foot are most suitable grown in hanging baskets. The basket is filled with the potting soil, to which coarse material such as charcoal is added, and is watered well. The section of fern is placed on the surface of the soil and held in position with pieces of wire bent into a U-shape and pushed into the soil over the stems. The stem is then just covered with soil, after which the fern is well watered. The newly potted plant should be kept in a shaded position for approximately a month.

Fixing to a Surface

Ferns such as Bird's Nest and Elkhorns may be fastened to a surface such as stone, well-seasoned hardwood timber, brick or other suitable surface. To enable the fern to become established, it should be tightly tied to the surface with nylon fishing line, old stockings or other material which will not rot. Sections of Elkhorn may be used as hanging subjects in shaded positions by passing a long piece of heavy gauge wire through the fern, then making a loop at the base to hold the wire in position, forming a hook at the other end. Plants attached to surfaces require more frequent watering than those grown in a pot.

Ferns Indoors

When ferns are to be grown indoors, select more robust types such as Fishbone Ferns (*Nephrolepis*), Mother Spleenwort or Bird's Nest Ferns. It is important to select a well lighted position but one which does not receive sun and is not subject to heat or drying air movement. A bathroom is usually an excellent position for an indoor fern. When the room is warm, it is essential to prevent drying of the ends of the fronds by spraying the fronds with a fine water spray, in addition to watering. Unless the indoor position is satisfactory, providing ideal conditions (a cool moist atmosphere) the fern should only be kept inside for limited periods. Having several plants which can be rotated for short periods indoors will assist in providing more attractive specimens.

Watering

Generally the same rules for watering previously described should be followed. However, as ferns have very soft foliage which dries out quickly unless a constant source of moisture is available, they require additional watering. A weekly soaking of the container in 5 to 7 cm of water for about an hour provides satisfactory conditions for their growth. It is important to keep the soil moist, but not wet, and this may entail daily watering during hot weather. To provide humid conditions, troughs of water may be kept in the vicinity of the ferns, while spraying with a fine water spray may be necessary several times a day during hot weather.

14. Growing Orchids

Australia has a great number of different kinds of orchids, but unfortunately many of them are not suitable for general cultivation. There are two chief groups: those that grow on trees and rocks (epiphytes) and those which grow in the ground (terrestrial).

Epiphytes

Found chiefly in rainforests and moist coastal valleys of the east coast, this group of orchids grow with their roots attached to the surface of trees and rocks. One type of tree-growing orchid, *Cymbidium*, grows with its roots in decayed wood in the hollow branches and trunks of trees. These orchids are often difficult to establish in cultivation. Among the tree and rock growing types, *Dendrobium* species and their hybrids are attractive and the easiest to cultivate and may be obtained from specialist native orchid nurseries. Those species from tropical and warm northern coastal areas require a heated glasshouse in southern areas. Where a bush house is available, species of *Sarchochilus*, such as *S. falcatus* (Orange Blossom Orchid), *S. hartmannii* and *S. fitzgeraldii* make beautiful specimen plants.

Terrestrial Orchids

This group of orchids, except for the two large growing types *Phaius* and *Calanthe*, consists of small orchids, usually with soft green leaves at ground level which die down each year to form tiny underground tubers, resembling a minute potato. Among the terrestrial orchids, *Phaius* and *Calanthe* and the Greenhoods (*Pterostylis*) are the easiest to grow. Generally terrestrial orchids are not readily available.

Growing Orchids in Pots and on Slabs

Epiphytic Types

Except for those orchids which naturally grow with some roots attached to the surface and a number growing free of the surface, such as the Orange Blossom Orchid (*Sarchochilus falcatus*), and small prostrate creeping types such as Tongue Orchid (*Dendrobium lingueforme*), most epiphytic orchids may be cultivated successfully in containers.

Potting Material Unlike plants which grow in the ground, epiphytic orchids require free circulation of air around the roots. Thus, potting material should consist of course substances such as pieces of charcoal, broken terracotta tiles or pots, and even pieces of foamed plastic, which do not pack tightly together.

Preparing the Potting Before an orchid is potted, any decayed, dead or broken roots and stems should be cut off. Frequently when orchids have been growing in a contaner where conditions have been unsatisfactory, it will be found when the orchid is removed from the pot that the roots in the middle of the plant are dead and rotted; these should be removed.

Division When the orchid is large or you wish to divide an existing orchid into two or more plants, divide it into sections containing at least six or seven stems.

In dividing the plant use sharp secateurs. First cut between the stems and carefully pull the plant apart. Cut off any damaged pieces and dust the cut surface with a fungicide. The divided pieces are then ready for potting. Many *Dendrobium* orchids develop small plants at the top of the stems. When these have developed roots they may be broken off and potted as separate plants. Placing several of these plants in the one pot makes a larger specimen.

Potting Potting is best carried out after flowering and before new growth commences, as this can be damaged during potting.

Select a container slightly larger than the piece of orchid to be potted. First check the drainage hole and then place pieces of terracotta or foamed plastic in the container to about one third the depth of the pot. Holding the orchid in the container, fill around the roots with the coarse material previously described until the pot is filled. Adjust the orchid to bring the base of the stems level with the top of the container and then firm the potting material, adding more if required. Water the plant well, adding Formula 20 to the water being used. Lightly sprinkle poultry manure over the potting material or water with Aquasol, Zest or a similar fertiliser. Then place the orchid in a protected position, but one with adequate light. Water daily to encourage growth.

Orchids on Slabs

Epiphytic orchids may be attached to the surface of a piece of well-seasoned hardwood, a cork slab, a section of tree fern trunk, branches of paperbark tree (*Melaleuca* species) or the outer surface of unglazed terracotta pots or agricultural pipes. Large growing orchids, such as *Dendrobium speciosum* and the tree-growing *D. speciosum* var. *hillii*, may be grown on a flat piece of asbestos cement supported by a wire frame.

Dendrobium lingueforme growing on the surface of a piece of hardwood paling.

Select the required slab, which should be large enough to allow the orchid to extend. Prepare the orchid as previously described and place in position on the slab, then fasten it tightly to the slab using nylon fishing line, pieces of old stocking or other material which will not rot. Attach a wire hook to the slab to enable it to be hung from a support. After fixing the plant, water it well with water to which Formula 20 and Aquasol or a similar fertiliser has been added. Place the orchid in a well lighted, protected position, preferably a bush house. Watering must not be neglected, as plants dry out quickly.

Cymbidium Orchids

These orchids are often difficult to establish and should be grown in a standard prepared orchid mix used for growing exotic cymbidiums, or in a mix of wood or leaf mould to which river sand has been added, ensuring that the pot is well drained. The use of fertilisers should be avoided.

Terrestrial Orchids

Potting Soil A similar soil mix to that recommended for ferns and rainforest plants, as previously discussed on page 00, is satisfactory for large orchids such as *Phaius* and *Calanthe* orchids. For small orchids, such as those which form small underground tubers, use a lighter soil mix similar to that given under Soil Mixes 1 and 2 on page 20.

Potting the Orchid

Large Orchids The plant may be divided into groups of two to three bulbs and any damaged roots should be cut off. A larger deep pot should be used and the plant placed in the position in which it is to grow.

Small Orchids with Tubers After placing drainage material in the pot, add potting soil to within 3 cm from the top and consolidate by watering. Place four to six small tubers in position and cover over with soil, water the pot well and place in a shaded protected position.

Cultivation

Selecting a Position

Epiphytes With some exceptions, orchids grow in rainforests and moist protected gullies where they receive at least broken sunlight or full sunlight for part of the day. Some species grow in more shaded locations. In selecting a position for orchids where a bush house is not available, ensure that the plant will receive at least 50% natural sunlight throughout the day. It is important to ensure that humidity is maintained and drying winds are avoided. This is particularly so with orchids growing on slabs as they dry out very rapidly. In drier areas the protection provided by a bush house or suitable screen may be required and in more southern areas a heated glass-house may be necessary if you wish to grow a number of different orchids.

Orchids growing in protected positions may be moved to more exposed positions during flowering, or taken indoors to display the flowers. Although the plants may have a setback and length of flowering be reduced, they will recover when moved back to their former position and the following year you will enjoy the flowers again.

Terrestrials With the exception of the orchid *Phaius,* which requires a well lighted position, ground orchids should be kept in a protected, part shaded position. Areas subject to drying winds should be avoided.

Watering

Epiphytes In their natural habitat, these orchids receive a plentiful supply of moisture from both rain and heavy dews which occur in rainforests at night. In cultivation rapid drying of the roots may occur due to the open nature of the potting mix and the free air circulation afforded by slabs.

Thus watering is required daily during the growing season, chiefly between October and March. As growth becomes less active, frequency of watering may be reduced to weekly or fortnightly during winter months. When watering is carried out it should be soaking; light watering should be avoided.

Terrestrials Large growing orchids such as *Phaius* and *Calanthe* should receive heavy watering during warm weather, when soil must be kept moist, but not wet. In hot dry locations this may entail daily watering. This frequency should be reduced to weekly during cold and winter weather. Small plants with underground tubers require watering every few days during the growing season and, when leaves die down, at least weekly, as the tubers only have a short resting period.

Fertilisers

Epiphytes Epiphytes should be fertilised regularly during the growing season. Where foliage fertilisers such as Aquasol are used, the fertiliser should be applied fortnightly, preferably together with a few drops of Formula 20. Alternatively, a light dusting of dry poultry manure may be applied monthly during the growing season. Irrespective of the type of ferti-liser used, heavy watering must not be neglected, otherwise burning of plants may occur.

Terrestrials The larger growing *Phaius* and *Calanthe* may be treated in the same manner as epiphytes during the growing season. For small tuber-forming orchids, a foliage spray every two months during the growing season is adequate.

Pests and Diseases

Orchids, like other plants, are attacked by various chewing insects, including the ubiquitous snails and slugs. A serious pest of *Dendrobium* orchids is an orange spotted beetle known as the Dendrobium Beetle which attacks the leaves and stems. The adult beetle also lays its eggs in the new growth; a soft grub develops which then destroys the stem. During the growing season it is important to spray at three-weekly intervals where there is beetle attack with a pesticide (see page 42).

Various fungi which can bring about rotting of stems, roots and leaves attack orchids requiring the use of a fungicide. An all-purpose spray will cope with both insect and fungal disease.

15. Disease and Pest Control

Plants in containers are subject to attack by various chewing, boring and sucking insects and by various fungal diseases. Action should be taken immediately any kind of attack occurs.

When using any type of chemical for controlling disease, it is vitally important to exercise care with its use. Avoid inhaling sprays, use protective clothing and wash the skin thoroughly after using chemicals. Clothing should be washed separately. Ensure that all chemical substances are used strictly in accordance with the manufacturer's instructions.

Insects

Chewing Insects

The grubs of many moths, wasps, adult beetles, grasshoppers and crickets may attack the tips and foliage of plants. Unless early attention is given, rapid complete defoliation of a plant may occur.

Control Grubs may be physically removed, preferably while you are wearing gloves, as some caterpillars can cause skin irritation. Control may also be achieved with sprays such as Malathion, Carbaryl or a general purpose spray used in accordance with the manufacturer's instructions.

Borers

Tip Borers The grubs of some moths bore into the tips of plants, killing the new growth.

Leaf Borers or Miners The larvae of various wasps and moths burrow into the tissue of leaves and stems, bringing about distortion and damage.

Galls A number of small wasps lay eggs in the stems and fruit of a number of plants. The small larvae live for some time in the tissue of the plants, causing a swelling called a gall, which, as well as being disfiguring, results in the stem dying or the seeds not forming.

Control Affected leaves and galls may be cut off and the plant sprayed with a systemic spray such as Lebaycid or Rogor in accordance with the manufacturer's directions. Spraying should be followed up with a further spray during development of new growth.

Sucking Insects

Various types of bugs, scales and thrips may suck the sap from the foliage and flower buds, resulting in considerable damage, particularly to new growth.

Control Aphis and scale insects may be physically removed using soapy water and a toothbrush. Take care when removing sucking bugs such as the Citrus Bug, as it can emit a fluid which, on contact, may cause damage to the eyes and skin. Mealy Bugs may be removed using a match with a cotton wool swab on the end which has been dipped in methylated spirits.

Spraying with insecticides such as Malathion, Carbaryl or similar substances will control these pests. When the infestation of scale is heavy, white oil should be added to the spray. Mealy Bug also affects the roots so the soil should be watered with Malathion at half the manufacturer's recommended strength, after first watering the plant.

Fungi and Nematodes

Various types of fungi and nematodes can attack the foliage and roots of plants. Root attack can be severe, commonly causing the loss of many plants. Foliage attack may be less severe, but may cause considerable damage.

Control The use of a suitable sterilised potting mix with good drainage is a most important measure against various root rots. It is important, however, for long-term cultivation of those plants prone to root rot (including many of the Western Australian species grown in Eastern states) to carry out a continuing programme to prevent loss by root diseases. As various root fungi become more active when soil temperatures rise to approximately 18°C and above, these control measures should be carried out from late spring to early autumn. Fungicides such as Terrazole and Fongarid applied to the soil in the container in accordance with the manufacturer's recommendation will give good control of the disease. Some members of the Banksia family (*Proteaceae*) may react unfavourably to Fongarid.

Foliage attack by fungi and leaf eelworm may be controlled by spraying with fungicides such as Captan, Diazinon and Benlate, or Lebaycid for leaf eelworm, whenever attack is observed.

16. Dried Plants for Floral Arrangements

For those who desire the beauty of Australian plants indoors, but are not prepared to attend to growing specimens, a number of different native species may be used in a dry state to make attractive floral arrangements.

Collection

Plant material for drying should only be collected in perfectly dry conditions, with no hint of moisture on leaves or flowers. The presence of excess moisture fosters the rapid growth of various fungi which mark and damage foliage and flowers.

The ideal time for the collection of plant material is on a hot sunny day about 2 to 3 p.m. Avoid dull moist days or mornings when dew is present on the foliage and flowers. In addition, the nectar in the flower is at its maximum in the morning and the high sugar content is conducive to the growth of fungi. As leaves can bruise easily, handle the collected material carefully.

Drying

Plant material may be dried very simply by hanging a loose bunch upside down in a well ventilated position. When surface moisture is present, the collected material should be spread out on several thicknesses of newspaper which will help to absorb the moisture. Change the paper twice a day and turn the foliage over to assist in drying out. After excess moisture has been removed, the collected material may be hung up to dry for three to four week. If the drying rate is too rapid, in a rather breezy area, foliage and flowers may become brittle and easily damaged. Wrapping the plant material with newspaper in the manner of a bunch of flowers will reduce the rate of drying.

Another method which is sometimes used is to stand the collected material for several days in about 3 cm of a mixture of glycerine and water, made up in proportions varying from 1:1 to 1:3 (1 glycerine, 3 water). Then the foliage is removed and dried in the usual manner. The glycerine tends to give a slight sheen to the foliage and can help retain colour.

Problems with Collected Flowers

Plants which produce a large quantity of nectar, such as Spider Flowers (*Grevillea*) and Bottlebrush (*Callistemon* and *Melaleuca*), lose their colour very rapidly and, being soft in texture, tend to shrivel and collapse when dried. An expensive method, but one which enables such flowers to retain shape and some colour, is to first shake them to remove excess nectar, then place them in a suitable box and cover with silica gel. After two or three days the flowers should be removed and placed in a fresh box of silica gel where they remain for approximately two to three weeks. Silica gel may be placed in an oven at low temperature for approximately five minutes to draw off moisture and may then be reused.

The flowers of the paper daisies *Helichrysum* and *Helipterum*, should be collected when they first open, as they continue to develop after picking. If the flowers are older, the centres of the flowers develop into seed heads, making them unsatisfactory for use.

Fruits and Seed Cases

There are many different types of seed cases and fruit (the seed surrounding seed case) which, with their attached foliage, make attractive additions to dried arrangements. Among the more readily obtainable are those of the *Banksia* family (Proteaceae) which have many attractive forms—the fruiting spikes vary in shape from globular to very large and cylindrical; the various woody fruits of *Hakea*, *Dryandra*, *Isopogon* and *Petrophile* species; fruit of *Brachychiton* species such as the Flame Tree and Kurrajong; among the Eucalypts, there is a wide range from groups of small fruits to large woody types; the She Oaks (*Casuarina* species), particularly some of the larger types; the fruiting seed heads of many different native grasses are also most attractive.

Fruits such as *Hakea*, *Casuarina* and Eucalypt open and release the seed after they are collected. The fruit of *Brachychiton* should be handled with care when they open as irritant hairs surround the seed.

Foliage

Among the Eucalypts, those types which keep their juvenile opposite foliage for indefinite periods are most attractive, especially *Eucalyptus cinerea*, *E. gunnii*, *E. kruseans* and *E. perreniana*. The many different forms of toothed leaves of the Proteacea family are also very attractive, for example *Dryandra* and *Banksia*.The sedge group, most of which grow in moist areas, may have stiff or curved stalks, often with small seeds; the fruiting spike of the Bulrush is also attractive.

Flowers

When selecting flowers for drying, those types which have papery petals and bracts, or those which do not sag as they dry, are the best ones to use. Among these Smoke Bush (*Conospermum* species), various paper daisies such as *Helichrysum* and *Helipterum*, Kangaroo Paws (*Anigozanthos* species) are among the more readily available types; various *Banksia* and *Dryandra* species are also suitable.

Storing Dried Material

Dried material must be kept perfectly dry at all times and when not on display must be stored carefully to prevent damage. Older dried material especially becomes very brittle. Placing the dried material in a large paper bag, or wrapping it with newspaper in the manner of a bunch of flowers, are simple ways to protect the material which should be hung in a safe, well ventilated position. Various insects may attack the dried material but naphthalene will act as a deterrent.

17. Growing Water Plants

Some of the smaller types of water plants make very interesting container subjects. They are not readily available from nurserymen and may have to be obtained from the wild, wherever they commonly occur. Water plants include various Nardoos (*Marsilea* species), Water Buttons (*Cotula coronopifolia*) and the floating fern *Azolla*.

Containers

Various types of vessels which will hold water, such as larger plastic icecream containers, larger ceramic vessels or even old cement tubs or cisterns, are suitable for cultivating water plants. Planter boxes lined with heavy black plastic with the corners folded and not cut may also be used. Plastic icecream containers and similar less appealing, but practical, containers may be placed inside more decorative pots and planter boxes. Clear plastic is best avoided, as green algae grow rapidly on the inner surfaces of such containers in the presence of light.

A simple bench in full sun with trays of *Dendrobium* orchids 'Helen' and 'Marie' and icecream containers with water plants *Marsilea, Ranunculus, Cotula* and sedges.

Container Sizes

About 5 to 7 cm of soil must be placed in the bottom of the container. When larger plants such as Water Lilies (*Nymphaea*) are to be grown, a depth of approximately 15 cm of soil is required. As these plants must be grown in full sun, the width of the container should be not less than 15 cm to reduce overheating. Where plastic icecream containers are used, the 2-litre and 4-litre sizes are most satisfactory. The smaller containers are 16 cm square and 10 cm deep, the larger ones 21 cm square and 12 cm deep. Water Lilies require larger containers such as large ceramic vessels, old cement tubs or even an old bath.

Planting

Any type of silty or heavy soil is generally suitable for growing water plants. To prepare for planting, place approximately 5 to 7 cm of soil in the selected container and consolidate well by bumping the container several times on a flat surface. Make holes in the soil in the middle of the container, as the plants tend to grow towards the edge, place the plants in position and firm the soil around the plant. Place the container in a sunny position and carefully fill with water. With floating plants such as *Azolla*, put approximately 2 cm of soil in the bottom of the container, fill it with water and place the small plants on the water.

Maintenance

Watering

Maintaining the water level is most important because, as well as losing water by normal evaporation, the plants transpire a considerable amount. In addition, the plants require well oxygenated water, which necessitates daily topping-up or watering on alternate days.

Plant Attention

Water plants are attacked by various chewing insects such as snails and must be kept under observation. Some species with creeping stems tend to creep towards the edges of the container and require periodic replanting, which entails, where required, replanting sections of the plant back into the centre of the container. Plastic containers have the disadvantage that they tend to break down due to the action of sunlight and require periodic replacement. When growing *Azolla*, which rapidly covers the surface of the water, some plants may have to be removed periodically.

Given the above simple attention, plus the removal of weeds, water plants may be grown in containers for indefinite periods.

18. Plant Lists

To assist in the selection of plants, the various types have been arranged into groups according to their general habits of growth. As with all types of plants, there may be variation in growth habits, but the group arrangements should serve as a general guide. The various heights given, particularly for larger growing types, are generally less than would be expected where the plant is growing in open ground with unlimited root space. Even the growth of large foliage trees, such as Silky Oaks, Lillypillies and Eucalypts, may be controlled by following the principles previously outlined.

The list of plants selected is representative of some of the colourful forms of the more readily grown native plants. Although most are available from specialist native plant nurseries, some may be more difficult to obtain.

The measurements for plants are given approximately for convenience. Here is a general guide to convert metric to imperial measurement for those who still prefer it:

15 cm	=	6 inches
20 cm	=	8 inches
25 cm	=	9 inches
30 cm	=	1 foot
60 cm	=	2 feet
1 m	=	3 feet
2 m	=	6 feet

In general, Australian native plants, excluding ferns and orchids, grow and flower best in full sun. However, a number will stand up to shaded conditions, and for the benefit of those readers who have no choice in the matter, I have listed on pages 78 and 79 those plants which will tolerate shaded conditions. The letter after each entry refers back to the main lists where a full description of the plant will be found.

A: Small Plants to 30 cm

Boronia polygalifolia: a small suckering plant to 15 cm with narrow, lance shaped leaves; flowers in spring, pink, four petalled.

Brachycome iberidifolia (Swan River Daisy): a small soft annual daisy to about 20 cm with narrow leaves; flowers in spring with white, pink or blue petals and a yellow centre.

Dampiera linearis: a suckering plant with a number of slender stems, 30 cm or more, with narrow leaves; flowers in spring, blue, in small clusters.

Dampiera rosmarinifolia: a suckering spreading plant, about 30 cm, with numerous stems and greyish-green pointed leaves; flowers in spring, blue, in clusters.

Dampiera stricta: A suckering plant with erect stems 30 cm or more with small, lance shaped leaves; flowers in spring, pale to dark blue with spreading petals. **Plate 61**

Helichrysum baxteri: a soft plant with a number of slender stems, 15 cm, narrow dark green leaves, greyish beneath; flowers in spring and summer with white spreading, papery, petal-like bracts and yellow centre.

Helipterum manglesii: a soft slender annual paper daisy to 30 cm, leaves greyish-green, round to heart shaped; flowers in spring with white to pink, papery, petal-like bracts and yellow to black centre.

Helipterum roseum: similar to *H. manglesii*, but petals narrow.

Hibbertia stellaris: a small plant with a number of slender stems, about 15 cm, leaves dark green, narrow; flowers in spring, orange, in profusion. **Plate 66**

Lechenaultia biloba (Blue Lechenaultia): a plant with a number of slender stems, sometimes suckering, to about 25 cm, with numerous narrow leaves; flowers blue, in spring. **Plates 3, 5**

Lechenaultia formosa (Red Lechenaultia): a small plant, erect to prostrate, to about 25 cm; leaves narrow, numerous; flowers in spring, various shades from red to orange. **Plates 3, 4**

Tetratheca ciliaris (Black-eyed Susan): a slender plant with fine hairs on stems, about 30 cm, leaves narrow; flowers in spring, bright purplish-pink with darker centre. **Plate 64**

Tetratheca ericifolia (Black-eyed Susan): a small plant with erect slender stem, 25 cm, leaves small, narrow; flowers in spring, purplish-pink with darker centre.

Tetratheca thymifolia (Black-eyed Susan): a small plant with a number of erect stems, to 30 cm, roundish leaves in groups around stems; flowers in spring, purplish-pink with darker centre.

B: Plants to 60 cm

Actinotus helianthi (Flannel Flower): a slender biennial to 60 cm with soft grey divided leaves; flowers in spring, small, in woolly heads with white, large, spreading, petal-like bracts. **Plate 63**

Astartea heterantha: an erect plant to 60 cm with a number of slender stems with very small oval leaves; flowers in spring, white to pink with 5 spreading petals.

Baeckea astarteoides: a bushy plant 60 cm or more, with slender arching stems and very small narrow leaves; flowers in spring, small, white to pink with 5 spreading petals.

Correa 'mannii': a bushy plant to about 60 cm with oval leaves; flowers in winter and spring, pink, tubular, pendulous.

Correa pulchella: an erect plant about 60 cm with light green, oblong, oval to egg shaped leaves; flowers winter to spring, tubular, pinkish-red to orange.

Eriostemon verrucosus (Fairy Waxflower): a spreading plant to 60 cm with rough, greyish-green, round to wedge shaped leaves; flowers in spring, white with 5 spreading petals; there are double-petalled forms.

Gompholobium heuglii (Wedge Pea): an erect plant, 60 cm, with leaves divided into 3 narrow pointed leaflets; large, yellow pea flowers in spring. **Plate 74**

Grevillea brownii: a spreading plant 60 cm or more with oval, dark green leaves; flowers in spring, bright red in clusters. **Plate 60**

Grevillea lanigera: a spreading plant, 60 cm, with soft, woolly, greyish-green, oval leaves; flowers chiefly in spring, pink with cream in clusters.

Guichenotia macrantha: an erect plant, 60 cm, with long, narrow, soft, greyish, hairy leaves; flowers in spring, pink, mauve, bell shaped.

Helichrysum bracteatum (Yellow Paper Daisy): a variable soft plant to 60 cm with dark green, broad, lance-shaped leaves; flowers spring and summer, large, yellow with stiff spreading papery bracts and yellow centre. **Plate 62**

Helichrysum bracteatum 'Dargan Hill Monarch': a selected form to 60 cm with greyish-green, lance shaped leaves; flowers spring and summer with yellow, stiff, spreading, papery bracts.

Helichrysum semipapposum: an herbaceous perennial to 60 cm, frequently suckering, with greyish stems and soft lance shaped leaves; flowers in spring and summer; yellow daisies in small round heads.

Melaleuca violacea: a spreading plant to about 60 cm, with small oval greyish-green leaves; flowers in spring, violet, in clusters along stem.

Pimelea ferruginea: a bushy plant 60 cm or more with numerous smooth oval leaves; flowers in spring, pink, small, with many in globular heads. **Plate 75**

Pimelea rosea: a slender erect plant 60 cm or more with light green narrow leaves; flowers in spring, pink, small, tubular with a number in globular heads.

Plectanthus argentatus: a bushy soft hairy plant to 60 cm with square stems and fleshy, broad, green to greyish-green leaves with rounded toothed edges; flowers chiefly in spring and summer, pale blue, in long spikes.

Prostanthera aspalathoides: an erect plant 60 cm or more with narrow, fine, light green leaves; flowers in spring, tubular, red, orange or yellow.

Prostanthera denticulata: a spreading plant to 60 cm with small rough oval leaves; flowers in spring, tubular, mauve to purple in small groups.

Pultenaea scabra: a bushy plant 60 cm or more with narrow oblong leaves; yellow clusters of pea flowers in spring.

Pultenaea villosa: a spreading pendulous plant 60 cm or more with small oval hairy leaves; yellow pea flowers, in clusters in spring. **Plate 78**

Swainsona galegifolia: an erect suckering plant to 60 cm with soft feathery leaves; pink pea flowers in spikes, in spring.

Symphionema montanum: an erect plant 60 cm or more with deeply divided leaves; flowers in spring, small, cream, in slender spikes.

Verticordia plumosa: an erect plant 60 cm or more with numerous fine, narrow, greyish-green leaves; flowers in spring, pink with feathery edges, in clusters. **Plate 69**

Verticordia chrysantha: a bushy plant 60 cm with narrow dark green leaves; flowers in spring, yellow with feathery edges, in clusters.

Xanthosia rotundifolia (Southern Cross): a soft herbaceous plant to 60 cm, with dark green, circular, toothed leaves; flowers in spring, white in a spreading cluster of four.

C: Plants 60 cm to 1 m

Acacia elata (Winged Wattle): a leafless plant with flattened winged stems to about 1 m; flowers in spring, yellow, globular heads.

Acacia drummondii: a bushy plant to about 1 m with slightly hairy, feathery leaves; flowers in spring, yellow, rod shaped.

Acacia lineata: a bushy plant 1 m or more, with stiff, narrow, dark green leaves; flowers in spring, yellow, globular heads.

Bauera rubioides (River Rose): a spreading plant 60 cm or more, with small oval leaflets grouped around the stem; flowers in spring, pink with spreading petals. **Plate 87**

Bauera sessiliflora (Showy Bauera): an erect spreading plant to about 1 m with slightly hairy leaflets grouped around stem; flowers in spring, bright purplish-pink with spreading petals. **Plate 88**

Boronia anemonifolia: a small spreading plant about 60 cm with small divided leaves; flowers small, pale pink, with 4 spreading petals.

Boronia crenulata: a slender plant 60 cm or more with stems becoming pendulous and small spoon shaped leaves; flowers in spring, pink with 4 spreading petals.

Boronia denticulata: an erect plant 1 m or more with narrow, light green leaves; flowers in spring, pink, with spreading petals. **Plate 65**

Boronia floribunda: a bushy plant about 60 cm with soft feathery leaves; flowers in spring, highly perfumed, pale pink with spreading petals.

Boronia fraseri: an erect plant with angular smooth stems and coarse feathery leaves; flowers in spring, pink with spreading petals.

Boronia fraseri* x *mollis: a vigorous hybrid with angular, slightly hairy stems and coarse feathery leaves; flowers in spring, pink with spreading petals.

1. *Hemiandra pungens* in a basket (p.73)

2. *Scaevola humilis* in a basket (p.73)

3. *Lechenaultia formosa* (orange prostrate) in a basket (p.47)

4. *Lechenaultia formosa* (orange upright) in a basket (p.47)

5. *Lechanaultia biloba* in a basket (p.47)

6. *Brachycome stuartii* in a basket (p.47)

7. *Hibbertia stellaris* (p.74)

8. *Lechanaultia biloba* (p.47)

9. *Helichrysum bracteatum* (p.48)

10. *Scleranthus biflorus* (p.74)

11. *Isotoma fluviatiles* (p.73)

12. *Boronia* species

13. *Boronia serrulata* (p.65)

14. *Boronia* species

15. *Boronia mollis* (p.65)

16. *Boronia denticulata* (p.48)

17. *Chorizema cordatum* (p.65)

18. *Rhododendron lochae* (p.68)

19. *Dryandra polycephala* (p.66)

20. *Ficus benjamina* (p.75)

21. *Callistemon salignus* (p.27)

22. *Lepidozamia peroffskyana* (p.78)

23. *Livistona australis*

23a. Group of *Livistona* species (p.78)

24. *Syzygium luehmannii* (p.76)

25. *Asplenium australasicum* in basket

26. *Asplenium australasicum*

27. *Blechnum minor*

28. *Davallia pixidata* in basket

29. *Asplenium bulbiferum*

30. *Cyathea cooperi*

31. *Dendrobium kingianum* var. *alba*

32. *Dendrobium lingueforme*

33. *Dendrobium speciosum* var. *hillii*, growing on a piece of asbestos cement

34. *Dendrobium* x *specio-kingianum* 'Helen'

35. *Dendrobium kingianum*

36. *Dendrobium kingianum*

37. *Sarcochilus fitzgeraldii*

38. *Sarcochilus hartmannii*

39. *Dendrobium teretifolium*

40. *Chamelaucium uncinatum* and *Boronia mollis* (pp.65–9)

41. *Prostanthera rhombea* (pink form) (p.68)

42. *Prostanthera ovalifolia* (p.71)

43. *Ceratopetalum gummiferum* (p.69)

44. *Callistemon* 'Hannah Ray', (p.69)

45. *Callistemon viminalis* (p.69)

46. *Grevillea biternata* (p.74)

47. *Pandorea jasminoides* (p.73)

48. *Pandorea pandorana* (white form) (p.73)

Water Plants (p.78)

49. *Azolla pinnata*

50. *Nymphoides geminatum*

51. *Marsilea drummondii*

52. *Marsilea mutica*

53. *Marsilea angustifolia*

Bonsai

54. *Rulingia hermanniifolia* (p.74)

55. *Banksia serrata* (p.69)

Dried Flowers

56. *Banksia aemula* (p.69)

57. Dried Banksias

58. Dried flowers: Banksia, Regelia, Smokebush, Dryandra

59. Dried flowers: Helipterum, Restio, Casuarina

60 *Grevillea brownii* (p.47)

61. *Dampiera stricta* (p.47)

62. *Helichrysum bracteatum* (p.48)

63. *Actinotus helianthi* (p.47)

64. *Tetratheca ericifolia* (p.47)

65. *Boronia floribunda* (p.48)

66. *Hibbertia stellaris* (p.74)

67. *Baeckea ramosissima*

68. *Dampiera cuneata*

69. *Verticordia plumosa* (p.48)

70. *Thomasia petalocalyx* (p.68)

71. *Eremophila maculata* (p.66)

72. *Melaleuca thymifolia* (p.67)

73. *Hypocalymma angustifolium* (p.77)

74. *Gompholobium huegelii* (p.47)

75. *Pimelea ferruginea* (p.48)

76. *Acacia aspera*

77. *Helichrysum elatum* (p.67)

78. *Pultenaea villosa* (p.48)

79. *Rhododendron lochae* (p.68)

80. *Phelabium squamulosum* (p.68)

81. *Dillwynia sericea* (p.65)

82. *Dillwynia retorta* (p.65)

83. *Darwinia citriodora* (p.65)

84. *Pomaderris lanigera* (p.68)

85. *Grevillea sericea* (p.66)

86. *Hakea purpurea* (p.67)

87. *Bauera rubioides* (p.48)

88. *Bauera sessiliflora* (p.48)

89. *Dryandra formosa* (p.65)

90. *Melaleuca fulgens* (p.67)

91. *Acacia ulicifolia* (p.68)

92. *Eriostemon myoporoides* (p.66)

93. *Diplolaena grandiflora* (p.65)

94. *Micromyrtus ciliata* (p.74)

95. *Grevillea oleoides* (p.66)

96. *Grevillea speciosa* (p.66)

97. *Pimelea ligustrina* (p.68)

98. *Calytrix tetragona* (p.65)

99. *Gompholobium latifolium* (p.66)

100. *Cassia odorata* (p.65)

101. *Melaleuca elliptica* (p.67)

102. *Melaleuca nematophylla* (p.67)

103. *Grevillea acanthifolia* (p.66)

104. *Hakea cinerea* (p.67)

105. *Melaleuca megacephala*

106. *Isopogon anemonifolia* (p.67)

107. *Prostanthera ovalifolia* (p.71)

108. *Acacia terminalis* (p.68)

109. *Grevillea banksii* (p.70)

110. *Acacia verticillata* (p.68)

111. *Calothamnus quadrifidus* var. *asper* (p.69)

112. *Prostanthera lasianthos* (p.71)

113. *Leptospermum flavescens* (p.70)

114. *Callistemon speciosus* (p.69)

115. *Grevillea johnsonii* (p.70)

116. *Grevillea rosmarinifolia* (p.70)

117. *Hovea lanceolata*

118. *Grevillea asplenifolia* (p.70)

119. *Grevillea longifolia*

120. *Grevillea* "Robin Gordon" (p.67)

121. *Tristania laurina* (p.76)

122. *Kunzea ambigua* (p.76)

123. *Macadamia integrifolia* (p.76)

124. *Elaeocarpus reticulatus* (p.69)

125. *Banksia marginata* (p.69)

126. *Banksia aemula* (p.69)

127. *Banksia ericifolia* (p.69)

128. *Syzygium wilsonii* (p.77)

129. *Grevillea hookerana* (p.70)

130. *Hakea bucculenta* (p.70)

131. *Emmenosperma alphitonioides* (p.75)

132. *Stenocarpus sinuatus* (p.76)

133. *Brachycome ciliaris* (p.73)

134. *Hibbertia diffusa* (p.74)

135. *Hibbertia vestita* (p.74)

136. *Myoporum debile* (p.73)

137. *Hemiandra pungens* (p.73)

138. *Scaevola aemula* (p.74)

139. *Grevillea thelymanniana* (p.74)

140. *Kennedia prostrata* (p.74)

141. *Orthrosanthus multiflorus* (p.72)

142. *Conostylis setigera* (p.71)

143. *Sowerbaea juncea* (p.72)

144. *Dianella caerulea*

145. *Thysanotus multiflorus* (p.72)

146. *Stypandra glauca* (p.72)

147. *Patersonia glabrata* (p.72)

148. *Anigozanthos humilis* (p.71)

149. *Anigozanthos rufus* (p.71)

150. *Cordyline rubra* (p.79)

151. *Crinum pedunculatum* (p.71)

152. *Passiflora cinnabarina* (p.73)

153. *Pandorea pandorana* (p.72)

154. *Pandorea jasminoides* (p.73)

155. *Clematis aristata* (p.72)

156. *Hibbertia dentata* (p.72)

157. *Sollya heterophylla* (p.73)

158. *Hardenbergia comptoniana* (p.72)

159. *Hardenbergia violacea* (p.72)

Boronia heterophylla (Red Boronia): an erect plant to about 1 m, with thin feathery leaves; flowers in spring, red with petals forming a cup shape.

Boronia megastigma (Brown Boronia): an erect plant 60 cm to 1 m with leaves in 3 narrow leaflets; flowers in spring, highly perfumed, various shades of brown to yellow, cup shaped.

Boronia mollis (Soft Boronia): an erect plant 1 m or more with soft woolly stems and coarse feathery leaves; flowers in spring, pink with spreading petals.

Boronia molloyae: a bushy plant 1 m or more with soft feathery leaves; flowers in spring, red, cup shaped.

Boronia pinnata: a bushy plant 1 m or more with feathery aromatic leaves; flowers in spring, pink in clusters, petals spreading.

Boronia serrulata (Native Rose): a slender plant 60 cm or more with light green, round to oval leaves; flowers in spring, highly perfumed, deep pink, cup shaped.

Brachysema lanceolatum (Swan River Pea): an erect plant, 60 cm to 1 m with broad, lance shaped leaves, green above, silvery beneath; large red pea flowers in spring.

Calocephalus brownii (Cushion Bush): a bushy plant 60 cm to 1 m with numerous slender greyish-silver intertwined stems and tiny leaves; flowers in spring, small, yellowish daisies without petals, in globular heads.

Calytrix fraseri: a spreading plant 60 cm to 1 m with narrow dark green leaves; flowers in spring, pinkish-purple with spreading petals and bright yellow stamens.

Calytrix tetragona: a bushy plant to 1 m or more with numerous narrow light green leaves; flowers in spring, white to pink with spreading petals. **Plate 98**

Cassia artemesioides (Silver Cassia): a bushy plant 1 m or more, with silvery-grey feathery leaves; flowers in spring and summer, yellow, in clusters.

Cassia odorata: an erect to spreading plant 60 cm to 1 m or more, with green feathery leaves; flowers in spring, yellow, in clusters. **Plate 100**

Chorizema cordatum (Heart-leaved Flame Pea): an erect plant 60 cm to 1 m with stiff heart shaped leaves; flowers in spring, orange-red, pea shaped, in short spikes. **Plate 17**

Chorizema ilicifolia (Holly-leaved Flame Pea): an erect plant 60 cm to 1 m with oval leaves with toothed margins; flowers in spring, orange-red, pea shaped, in long spikes.

Correa aemula: a bushy plant 60 cm to 1 m with woolly stems and oval to egg shaped leaves; flowers in spring, green, tubular, pendulous.

Correa alba: a bushy plant 60 cm to 1 m with greyish-green, oval to round, thick leaves; flowers in spring, white, cup shaped.

Correa baeuerlenii (Chef's Cap Correa): an erect plant 60 cm to 1 m or more with shiny elliptical to lance shaped leaves; flowers autumn, winter, tubular, yellowish-green with flattened enlarged calyx.

Correa reflexa: a variable spreading to erect plant 60 cm or more with rough oblong to egg shaped leaves; flowers winter, spring, tubular, green to red with green top.

Crowea exalata (Pink Waxflower): an erect plant with narrow lance shaped leaves; flowers autumn, winter, pink with 5 spreading petals.

Crowea saligna (Pink Waxflower): an erect plant 60 cm or more with fleshy aromatic lance shaped leaves; flowers autumn, winter, pink with spreading petals.

Dampiera purpurea: an erect slender plant to 1 m with rough, greyish-green, oval to round leaves; flowers in spring, blue to purplish-pink with spreading petals.

Darwinia citriodora (Lemon-scented Darwinia): a bushy shrub, 1 m, with neatly arranged, lemon-scented, greyish to bluish-green oval leaves; flowers in winter and spring, red with green in small pin-cushion heads. **Plate 83**

Dillwynia floribunda (Eggs and Bacon): an erect plant to 1 m with crowded narrow dark green leaves; flowers spring, yellow with red pea flowers in spikes.

Dillwynia retorta (Eggs and Bacon): a bushy plant 1 m with narrow leaves; yellow with red pea flowers in clusters in spring. **Plate 82**

Dillwynia sericea (Showy Parrot Pea): a bushy plant with narrow, hairy, greyish-green leaves; orange to pink pea flowers in short spikes in spring. **Plate 81**

Diplolaena angustifolia: similar to *D. grandiflora* (below) with narrower felty leaves.

Diplolaena grandiflora: an erect bushy shrub 1 m or more with dark green, broad, lance shaped leaves; flowers in spring, red with conspicuous stamens, a number of flowers with bracts in a pendulous head. **Plate 93**

Dryandra formosa: a bushy spreading plant 1 m with long, narrow, deeply toothed leaves; flowers in spring, orange, in dense globular heads. **Plate 89**

Dryandra polycephala: an erect plant to 1 m, with very narrow, sharply toothed leaves; flowers in spring, yellow, in dense heads. **Plate 19**

Dryandra sessilis: a bushy plant to 1 m with broad, toothed, wedge-shaped leaves; flowers in spring, yellow, in dense heads.

Epacris impressa (Common Heath): an erect slender plant 60 cm or more with stem-clasping, pointed leaves; flowers in spring, tubular, red, pink or white, at upper ends of branches.

Epacris longiflora (Native Fuchsia): a straggling plant 60 cm to 1 m with stem-clasping, sharply pointed leaves; flowers in spring, tubular, long, red with white tip.

Eremophila maculata: a spreading shrub, 60 cm, with lance shaped leaves; flowers in spring, various shades of red, also yellow, tubular, with spreading lobes. **Plate 71**

Eriostemon difformis: an erect plant, 60 cm to 1 m, with narrow dark green leaves; flowers in spring, white, with spreading petals. **Plate 66**

Eriostemon myoporoides (Native Daphne): a bushy plant 1 m or more with greyish green, long to short, lance shaped leaves; flowers in spring, white, with 5 spreading petals. **Plate 92**

Eriostemon nodiflorus: a slender plant, 60 cm, with soft, narrow leaves; flowers in spring, in slender spikes of mauve.

Eriostemon spicatus: an erect slender plant, 60 cm, with very narrow leaves; flowers in spring, pink to mauve, in slender spikes.

Eutaxia obovata: an erect shrub, 60 cm to 1 m, with light green, oblong, pointed leaves; orange with reddish-brown pea flowers, in spring.

Gompholobium grandiflorum (Wedge Pea): an erect plant with leaves in 3 narrow pointed leaflets; flowers in spring, large, yellow, pea shaped.

Gompholobium latifolium (Glory Wedge Pea): an erect plant 1 m or more, with leaves having 3 long leaflets; flowers in spring, large, yellow, pea shaped. **Plate 99**

Grevillea acanthifolia: an erect shrub 1 m or more with sharply pointed, deeply lobed leaves; flowers in spring, red, arranged in a toothbrush fashion. **Plate 103**

Grevillea alpina: a variable plant, from spreading to erect, 60 cm to 1 m or more, with oval leaves; flowers in spring, orange to pink and red with white, in clusters.

Grevillea aquifolium (Holly Grevillea): a straggling to bushy plant 60 cm to 1 m or more with stiff oblong leaves with spiny edges; flowers in spring, green with red, arranged in a toothbrush manner.

Grevillea baueri: a bushy plant 60 cm to 1 m with numerous oblong to oval leaves; flowers in spring, pink with white, in clusters.

Grevillea buxifolia (Grey Spider Flower): an erect bushy plant 1 m or more with hairy oval leaves; flowers in spring, grey, woolly, with brown, in clusters.

Grevillea capitellata: a variable bushy plant, 60 cm to 1 m, with narrow to broad, lance shaped leaves; flowers in spring, pink to dark red, in globular pendulous heads.

Grevillea chrysophaea (Golden Grevillea): a bushy hairy plant to 1 m with oblong to oval leaves; flowers in spring, yellow, hairy, in clusters.

Grevillea deilsiana: an erect plant 1 m or more with leaves divided into pointed segments; flowers in spring, yellow to red, in clusters.

Grevillea dimorpha (Flame Grevillea): a spreading to erect plant, 60 cm to 1 m or more, with long, narrow to broad, lance shaped leaves; flowers in spring, bright red, in clusters.

Grevillea floribunda: a bushy plant to 1 m with greyish-green, elliptical leaves; flowers in spring and summer, yellow, in clusters, covered with rusty hairs.

Grevillea juniperina: usually an erect, bushy, prickly plant 1 m or more, leaves narrow, sharply-pointed; flowers in spring, yellow to orange, in clusters.

Grevillea lavendulacea: a variable plant, erect to spreading, 60 cm to 1 m or more, with narrow to broad, green to greyish leaves; flowers in spring, bright red, in clusters.

Grevillea oleoides: an erect plant 1 m or more with long, narrow to broad, dark green leaves, greyish beneath; flowers in spring, bright red, in clusters.

Grevillea pinaster: an erect bushy plant 1 m or more with greyish-green leaves divided into 3 narrow leaflets; flowers in winter to spring, red with white, in one-sided pendulous clusters.

Grevillea sericea (Pink Grevillea): a variable plant, 1 m or more, with oval shaped leaves; flowers chiefly in spring, pale to deep pink, in clusters.

Grevillea speciosa (Red Grevillea): a spreading to erect plant, 1 m or more, with elliptical to narrow, lance shaped leaves; flowers in spring, red, in clusters.

Grevillea: Hybrids and selected forms: There are numerous different types, the most outstanding being 'Robyn Gordon', which is a bushy plant 1 m or more with deeply divided leaves and large long clusters of red flowers, over an extended period; the 'Poorinda' hybrids are large bushy plants 1 m or more with flowers red, orange to apricot, the older 'Crosbie Morrison' with red flowers; among the larger newer hybrids, with deeply divided leaves, are 'Dusky Pink' with large pink flowers and 'Ned Kelly' with large, red with yellow flowers.
Hakea cinerea: a bushy plant 1 m or more with stiff, grey-green leaves; flowers in spring, yellow to brownish in pincushion clusters. **Plate 104**
Hakea purpurea: a bushy plant to 1 m with divided forked leaves; flowers in spring, red, in clusters. **Plate 86**
Helichrysum elatum (White Paper Daisy): a slender, erect perennial, 60 cm to 1 m, with soft, broad, grey, lance shaped leaves; flowers in spring and summer with white spreading papery bracts. **Plate 77**
Hypocalymma angustifolium: a plant with a number of slender stems, 60 cm, with narrow leaves; flowers in spring, white to pale pink, with several in fluffy clusters. **Plate 73**
Hypocalymma cordatum: a bushy plant 60 cm or more with stem-clasping, heart shaped leaves; flowers white, in fluffy clusters.
Hypocalymma robustum (Swan River Myrtle): an erect slender shrub, 60 cm, with dark green narrow leaves; flowers in spring, rosy-pink, in fluffy clusters.
Indigofera australis (Austral Indigo): a bushy plant to 1 m with soft feathery leaves; purplish-pink pea flowers in slender sprays.
Isopogon anemonifolius (Drumstick): a bushy plant 60 cm or more with leaves divided into a number of stiff segments; flowers in spring, yellow, in globular heads. **Plate 106**
Isopogon anethifolius: an erect plant to 1 m with leaves divided into a number of narrow segments; flowers in spring, yellow, in dense globular heads.
Isopogon latifolius: an erect plant with stiff, broad, oblong leaves; flowers in spring, pink, in large globular heads.
Kunzea parvifolia: an erect to spreading plant with very small stem-clasping leaves; flowers in spring, purplish-pink in soft fluffy heads.
Lasiopetalum behrii: a bushy plant to 1 m, with woolly, long, greyish-green, oblong leaves; flowers in spring, cream with pink, in drooping clusters.
Leptospermum rotundifolium: a bushy plant to 1 m or more with shiny round pointed leaves; flowers in spring, pale to purple-pink, large, with 5 spreading petals.
Melaleuca coccinea (Goldfields Bottlebrush): a bushy shrub, 1 m, with stem-clasping, green, oval leaves; flowers in summer, bright red, in small branches.
Melaleuca elliptica (Oval-leaf Honey Myrtle): a bushy plant 1 m or more with greyish-green oval leaves; flowers spring and summer, crimson, in bottlebrush spikes. **Plate 101**
Melaleuca fulgens (Scarlet Honey Myrtle): an erect plant, 1 m, with narrow, lance shaped leaves; flowers in spring, red, in bottlebrush spikes. **Plate 9**
Melaleuca glaberima: a spreading plant, 60 cm, with slender short leaves; flowers in spring, pink, in small bottlebrush spikes.
Melaleuca nematophylla: an erect shrub, 1 m or more, with needle-like leaves; flowers in spring, pink, in globular heads. **Plate 102**
Melaleuca pulchella (Claw Flower): a slender erect plant, 60 cm, with small, greyish-green, oval leaves; flowers in spring, pink, in claw shaped clusters.
Melaleuca radula (Graceful Honey Myrtle): an erect slender plant with narrow greyish-green leaves; flowers in spring, mauve, in small bottlebrush spikes.
Melaleuca scabra (Rough Honey Myrtle): a bushy plant to 60 cm with narrow, small, rough leaves; flowers in spring, deep pink in small heads.
Melaleuca steedmanii: an erect bushy plant, 1 m, with greyish-green elliptical leaves; flowers in spring, scarlet, in bottlebrush spikes.
Melaleuca thymifolia: an erect bushy plant to 60 cm or more with narrow, oval, greyish-green leaves; flowers spring and summer, mauve, in claw-like clusters. **Plate 72**
Melaleuca violacea: a spreading plant, 60 cm or more, with small, greyish-green, oval leaves; flowers in spring.
Melaleuca wilsonii: a spreading plant, 60 cm or more, with narrow, stiff, greyish-green leaves; flowers in spring, mauve, in clusters along stem.
Olearia elliptica (Sticky Daisy Bush): an erect bushy daisy plant, 1 m or more, with elliptical, sticky, dark green leaves; flowers in spring and summer, in terminal clusters, white, small, with spreading petals and yellow centre.

Olearia phlogopappa: an erect bush 1 m or more with soft, greyish-green, oblong leaves; flowers in spring and summer, in clusters, white to pale pinkish-blue with spreading petals and yellow centre.
Olearia ramulosa: a slender erect bushy plant, 1 m or more, with very small, thick leaves; flowers in spring and summer, small, in clusters, with white spreading petals and yellow centre.
Olearia tomentosa: an erect bushy plant, 60 cm to 1 m, with broad, oval, woolly, slightly toothed leaves; flowers in spring and summer, large, white to pale blue with spreading petals.
Phebalium squamulosum: a bushy plant to 1 m with oblong leaves; green above and greyish beneath; flowers in spring, small, yellow, in terminal heads. **Plate 80**
Pimelea ligustrina: a bushy plant to 1 m or more, with light green, broad, lance shaped leaves; flowers in spring, white, small, in dense globular heads. **Plate 97**
Pomaderris lanigera: a bushy plant to 1 m with soft, felty, oval leaves; flowers in spring, bright yellow, in clusters. **Plate 84**
Prostanthera incisa: a spreading plant, 1 m, with strongly aromatic, coarsely toothed, finely hairy leaves; flowers in short sprays, mauve.
Prostanthera nivea var. ***induta:*** an erect plant, 1 m or more, leaves narrow, greyish-green; flowers in spring, large, lavender, in leaf axils. **Plate 68**
Prostanthera nivea: similar to the var. *induta*, but flowers white and leaves green.
Prostanthera prunelloides: an erect plant, 1 m or more, with large, soft, round to egg-shaped leaves; flowers in spring, white to pale blue in spikes.
Prostanthera rhombea: a slender plant, 60 cm to 1 m, with small round to rhomboid-shaped leaves; flowers in spring, mauve, in leaf axils. **Plate 41**
Prostanthera scutellarioides: a spreading plant to 1 m with small, smooth, oval leaves; flowers in spring, mauve to violet, in leaf axils.
Rhododendron lochae: a bushy spreading plant, 60 cm to 1 m, with shiny, thick, oval, dark green leaves; flowers in summer, large, shiny, deep red, waxy bells in clusters. **Plates 18, 79**
Templetonia retusa: an erect plant to 1 m with greyish-green, wedge shaped leaves; flowers winter and early spring, large pea flowers, pink to red.
Thomasia petalocalyx: a bushy plant, 60 cm to 1 m, with hairy oval leaves; flowers in spring, pinkish-mauve, in clusters. **Plate 70**
Thryptomene saxicola (also includes 'Payne's hybrid'): a bushy plant, 60 cm to 1 m, with arching branches, numerous small oval leaves; flowers chiefly autumn to spring, small, pink in upper leaf axils.

D: Larger Plants from 1 m to 2.5 m

Acacia (the term "leaves" is used in lieu of "phyllodes".)
Acacia acinacea (Gold Dust Wattle): a spreading plant, 1 m or more, with small narrow leaves; flowers in spring, in bright yellow, ball shaped heads.
Acacia armata (Hedge Wattle): a bushy plant to 2 m with spiny stems and pointed oblong leaves; flowers in spring in golden yellow, ball shaped heads.
Acacia brownii: an erect plant 1 m or more with small needle-like leaves; flowers in spring, in golden yellow heads.
Acacia buxifolia (Box-leaf Wattle): an erect bushy plant to 2 m with small, broad, oval leaves; flowers in spring, in sprays of bright yellow balls.
Acacia decora: an erect plant, 1 to 2 m, with greyish-green, narrow, lance shaped leaves; flowers in spring, in sprays of bright yellow heads.
Acacia myrtifolia: a bushy plant, 1 to 2 m, with thick, broad, lance shaped leaves; flowers in spring, in short sprays of pale yellow heads.
Acacia suaveolens (Sweet-scented Wattle): an erect slender plant, 1 to 2 m, with lance shaped leaves; flowers late winter, in short sprays of pale yellow globular heads.
Acacia terminalis: an erect bushy plant to 2 m with feathery leaves; flowers in autumn to early spring, in sprays of yellow heads. **Plate 108**
Acacia verticillata: an erect plant, 2 m, with needle-like leaves in groups around stems; flowers in spring in yellow rods. **Plate 110**
Acacia vestita: a bushy pendulous plant, 2 m, with soft, greyish, pointed, egg shaped leaves; flowers in spring in sprays of yellow heads.
Acacia ulicifolia (Prickly Moses): a shrub very similar to *A. brownii*, but flowers cream and leaves more slender.
Baeckea virgata: an erect bushy plant, 2 m, with numerous small, dark green, oval leaves; flowers in summer, small, white with spreading petals.
Banksia aemula (syn. *B. serratifolia*): a large bushy plant, 2 m or more, with long, narrow, elliptical, toothed leaves; flowers autumn, yellow, in large dense spikes. **Plates 56, 126**

Banksia ashbyi: a bushy plant, 2 m, with long toothed leaves; flowers late winter to spring, in orange dense spikes.

Banksia aspleniifolia (now *B. oblongifolia*): a bushy plant with leathery, coarsely toothed leaves; flowers in autumn and winter, in dense yellowish-green spikes.

Banksia baxteri: a bushy plant to 2 m with narrow, attractively toothed leaves; flowers in spring, yellow, in dome-shaped spikes.

Banksia caleyi: a bushy plant to 2 m with broad, coarsely toothed leaves; flowers in spring and summer, reddish, dense, pendulous spikes.

Banksia collina: a bushy spreading plant, 1 to 2 m, with small, narrow, finely toothed leaves; flowers in autumn and winter, orange to bronze, in long dense spikes.

Banksia ericifolia (Heath-leaf Banksia): a large spreading plant, 2 m or more, with small, narrow, light green leaves; flowers autumn to winter, golden, in large dense spikes. **Plate 127**

Banksia marginata: a bushy spreading plant, 2 m, with long narrow leaves, green above, greyish beneath; flowers autumn and winter, in small yellow dense spike. **Plate 125**

Banksia robur: a spreading plant, 1 to 2 m, with large, broad, toothed leaves; flowers winter, spring.

Banksia serrata: a large spreading plant, 2.5 m or more, with leathery, long, wedge shaped, coarsely toothed leaves; flowers late summer and autumn, greyish to yellow, in large dense spikes. **Plate 55**

Banksia spinulosa: a spreading plant, 1 to 2 m, with long narrow leaves; flowers in winter, yellow to bronze, in long dense spikes.

***Callistemon* 'Captain Cook':** a bushy plant, 2 m, with narrow, lance shaped leaves; flowers late spring, red, in small bottlebrush spikes.

Callistemon citrinus (Crimson Bottlebrush): a bushy plant to 2 m with stiff, lance shaped leaves; flowers in late spring, crimson, in large bottlebrush spikes.

***Callistemon* 'Endeavour':** a bushy plant to 2 m with lance shaped leaves; flowers in spring, crimson, in large bottlebrush spikes.

***Callistemon* 'Gawler Hybrid'** or **'Harkness':** a bushy plant, 2 m, with large, lance shaped leaves; flowers in late spring, crimson, in very large bottlebrush spikes.

***Callistemon* 'Hannah Ray':** similar to *C.* 'Captain Cook' but of larger growth. **Plate 44**

Callistemon linearis (Narrow-leaf Bottlebrush): a stiff plant with narrow, stiff leaves; flowers in spring, red, in large bottlebrush spikes.

Callistemon pinifolius (Green Bottlebrush): a bushy plant to 2 m with very narrow, stiff leaves; flowers in spring, green, in small bottlebrush spikes.

***Callistemon* 'Reeves Pink':** a bushy plant to 2 m with lance shaped leaves; flowers late spring, pink, in large bottlebrush spikes.

Callistemon speciosus: an erect plant, 2 m, with thick, oblong, grey-green leaves; flowers late spring, bright red with yellow anthers, in long dense bottlebrush spikes. **Plate 114**

Callistemon viminalis: a large bushy plant to 3 m with lance shaped leaves, flowers in spring, red pendulous bottlebrush spikes. **Plate 45**

Calothamnus asper: a bushy spreading shrub, 1 to 1.5 m, with small, narrow, flattened leaves; flowers spring, bright red bottlebrush clusters. **Plate 111**

Calothamnus quadrifidus (Common Net-bush): a bushy spreading plant to 1.5 m with very narrow, greyish-green leaves; flowers in spring, red, in one-sided bottlebrush spikes.

Calothamnus sanguineus: a spreading plant 1 m or more, with soft needle-like leaves; flowers in spring, red, in one-sided spikes.

Calothamnus villosus: a bushy plant 1 to 2 m with hairy, soft, needle-like leaves; flowers in spring, red, with yellow anthers, in bottlebrush spikes.

Ceratopetalum gummiferum (New South Wales Christmas Bush): a bushy plant, 2 m, with leaves divided into 2 spreading leaflets; flowers in spring followed by fruit with 5 red, spreading, calyx segments. **Plate 43**

Chamelaucium uncinatum (Geraldton Wax): a bushy shrub to 2 m with numerous narrow, soft leaves; flowers in spring, white to red, with 5 waxy spreading petals. **Plate 40**

Daviesia corymbosa: an erect plant, 1 m or more, with long leaves; yellow with red pea flowers in clusters in spring.

Daviesia latifolia: an erect plant, 1 to 2 m, with tough broad wavy leaves; small yellow pea flowers with red, in clusters in spring.

Elaeocarpus reticulatus (Blueberry Ash): a slow-growing bushy plant to 2.5 m with elliptical leaves; flowers spring, white, bell-shaped, with fringed margin, followed by blue berries. **Plate 124**

Elaeocarpus reticulatus "pink": a pink-flowered form, 1 to 2 m.

Grevillea aspleniifolia: a large spreading plant to 2 m, with long narrow, entire or toothed leaves; flowers in spring, red, in one sided sprays. **Plate 118**

Grevillea banksii: an erect plant, 2 m, with large, feathery leaves; flowers bright red or white, in terminal spikes. **Plate 109**

Grevillea brevicuspis: a bushy plant, 1 to 2 m, with sharply pointed, divided leaves; flowers in spring, white, in clusters.

Grevillea glabrata: a large bushy plant with smooth, greyish-green, lobed leaves; flowers in spring, white, in clusters.

Grevillea hookerana: a large spreading plant, 2 m, with large, finely divided leaves; flowers in spring, red, in one sided sprays. **Plate 129**

Grevillea johnsonii: a bushy plant to 2 m with leaves divided into long, narrow segments; flowers in winter and spring, orange with red, in clusters.

Grevillea longistylis: a bushy plant very similar to *G. johnsonii.*

Grevillea rosmarinifolia: a bushy spreading plant, 1 to 2 m, with numerous crowded, sharply pointed leaves; flowers in spring, pink with white, in clusters.

Hakea bucculenta: an erect bushy plant, 2 m, with long narrow, flat leaves with a distinct central vein; flowers in spring, deep pink to red, in long spikes. **Plate 130**

Hakea coriacea: similar to *H. bucculenta*, but leaves broader with 9 to 10 distinct veins.

Hakea francissiana: similar to *H. bucculenta*, but leaves broader with 5 to 7 distinct veins.

Hakea multilineata: similar to *H. bucculenta*, but leaves much broader with many distinct veins.

Hakea laurina: a large bushy shrub, 2 m, sometimes with pendulous branches; flowers in spring, white with pink, in pincushion heads.

Hibiscus diversifolius: a spreading plant to 2 m, with oblong to round, dark green leaves; flowers spring and summer, large, yellow, with dark reddish-brown centre.

Hibiscus splendens: a large spreading plant to 2 m with grey, hairy, lobed leaves; flowers late spring, large, pink with deep red centre.

Hovea acutifolia: an erect plant, 1 to 2 m, with lance shaped leaves; bluish-purple pea flowers in spring.

Hovea elliptica: an erect plant, 1 to 2 m, with oblong to blunt elliptical leaves; purple pea flowers in spring.

Hovea lanceolata: an erect plant, 2 m, with broad lance shaped leaves; bluish-purple pea flowers in early spring. **Plate 117**

Kunzea ambigua: a bushy shrub to 2 m with pendulous branches and small narrow leaves; flowers late spring, white, in fluffy clusters. **Plate 122**

Kunzea baxteri: an erect bushy plant to 2 m with small, lance shaped leaves; flowers in spring, red bottlebrush spikes; takes some years to flower.

Kunzea pulchella: a bushy plant, 1 to 2 m, with oval, greyish-green leaves; flowers in spring, bright red, in fluffy clusters.

Leptospermum flavescens (Tantoon Teatree): a bushy plant, 2 m, with small, lance shaped leaves; flowers in spring, green, with 5 spreading petals. **Plate 113**

Leptospermum laevigatum (Coastal Teatree): a large spreading plant, 2 m, with greyish-green, elliptical leaves; flowers in late spring, white, with spreading petals.

Leptospermum petersonii (Lemon-scented Teatree): a large bushy plant, 2 m or more, with small, lance shaped, lemon-scented leaves; flowers in spring, white, with spreading petals.

Leptospermum sericium: an erect bushy shrub to 2 m with greyish-green, oval leaves; flowers in spring, large, pale to deep pink.

Leptospermum squarrosum (Peach-blossom Teatree): an erect straggling plant to 2 m with stiff, pointed leaves; flowers in spring, large, white to pink, with spreading petals.

Melaleuca decussata: an erect plant, 1 to 2 m, with neatly arranged, greyish-green leaves; flowers in spring, in small, mauve bottlebrush spikes.

Melaleuca hypericifolia: a bushy plant, 1 to 2 m, with light green, oval leaves; flowers in spring and summer, red, in bottlebrush spikes.

Melaleuca incana: a bushy pendulous plant to 2 m with small, soft, hairy, greyish-green leaves; flowers in spring, yellow, in small bottlebrush spikes.

Melaleuca lateritia (Robin Redbreast Bush): an erect plant, 1.5 to 2 m, with narrow leaves; flowers in spring, orange-red in bottlebrush spikes.

Melaleuca linariifolia: an erect bushy plant, 2.5 m, with papery bark and long, narrow leaves; flowers spring and summer, white, in bottlebrush spikes.

Melaleuca nodosa: an erect plant, 1 to 2 m, with narrow, stiff, pointed leaves; flowers in spring, pale yellow in fluffy heads.

Melaleuca squamea: an erect plant to 2 m with stem-clasping, heart shaped leaves; flowers in spring, pink, in tufted heads.
Pittosporum revolutum: a bushy spreading plant to 2 m with broad, elliptical, slightly hairy leaves; flowers in spring, yellow, bell shaped, followed by large yellow fruit.
Prostanthera lasianthos (Victorian Christmas Bush): a large erect plant, 2 m or more, with large, dark green, broad-toothed lance shaped leaves; flowers in late spring to summer, white with purple-spotted throat, in sprays. **Plate 112**
Prostanthera ovalifolia (Purple Mintbush): an erect plant to 2 m with lance shaped leaves, entire or toothed edges; flowers in spring, purple, in short sprays. **Plate 42**
Prostanthera rotundifolia: an erect plant, 1 to 2 m, with round to oval leaves; flowers in spring, violet, lilac, mauve to pink, in short sprays.
Prostanthera sieberi: a spreading plant to 2 m with strongly aromatic, oblong to egg shaped, coarsely toothed leaves; flowers in spring, pale mauve to violet, in short sprays.
Westringia brevifolia: an erect bushy plant, 1 to 2 m, with oval, green-greyish leaves; flowers in spring, pale lilac.
Westringia fruticosa (Coast Rosemary): a bushy plant, 1 to 2 m, with greyish leaves; flowers in spring, white, in pairs.

E: Tufted and Clump-forming Plants with Strap or Grass-like Leaves

Anigozanthos flavidus (Albany Kangaroo Paw): a vigorous growing plant, leaves dark green, strap-like to 60 cm; flowers in late spring, tubular, yellow to green or reddish on long stems to 120 cm.
Anigozanthos humilis (Cat's Paw): a small plant with short, flat, greyish-green, often curved leaves, 15 to 70 cm long; flowers tubular, in sprays, yellow, orange to reddish, woolly, on stems to 70 cm. **Plate 148**
Anigozanthos manglesii (Red and Green Kangaroo Paw): a rapid growing, often short-lived plant, leaves light green, strap-like; flowers in spring, tubular, green with red base on stalk to 60 cm.
Anigozanthos preissii (Albany Cat's Paw): a small plant with light green strap leaves to 30 cm; flowers in spring, yellow, with green and red on stems to 90 cm.
Anigozanthos pulcherrimus (Golden Kangaroo Paw): a plant with light green strap leaves, 30 to 60 cm; flowers in spring, golden, in heads, on woolly red stalks to 90 cm.
Anigozanthos rufus (Red Kangaroo Paw): a vigorous plant; leaves dark green, slightly woolly and finely toothed; flowers in spring, red, woolly, on stem to 90 cm. **Plate 149**
Anigozanthos viridis (Green Kangaroo Paw): a small plant with narrow strap leaves to 30 cm; flowers in spring, light to yellowish green, on stems to 60 cm.
Selected types: There are a number of selected types of the above and some hybrids.
Blandfordia grandiflora (Christmas Bell): a plant with stiff, dark green, grass-like leaves to 30 cm; flowers in spring, bell shaped, red with yellow tips on stem to 60 cm.
Blandfordia nobilis (Christmas Bell): a plant with stiff, dark green, grass-like leaves; flowers in spring, tubular, red with yellow tips.
Bulbine bulbosa (Bulbine Lily): a small plant with soft, onion-like leaves, about 15 cm; flowers yellow, in spikes to 45 cm.
Burchardia umbellata (Milkmaids): a small plant with soft, narrow, strap leaves to about 15 cm; flowers in spring, creamish-pink, on short sprays to 15 cm.
Conostylis aculeata: a tufted plant with yellowish-green strap leaves, about 30 cm; flowers in spring, small, yellow, in heads, on stems to 45 cm.
Conostylis setigera: a low-growing, spreading, tufted plant with narrow leaves, to 15 cm; flowers in spring, small, in heads, on stems to 15 cm. **Plate 142**
Conostylis stylidioides: a small, tufted, spreading plant with narrow leaves, about 5 cm, and forming aerial roots which hold tufts clear of the ground; flowers in spring, small, yellow, in heads on stems 10 to 15 cm.
Crinum pedunculatum (Swamp Lily): a large plant with large, broad, long, fleshy leaves, 1 to 1.5 m long; flowers spring to summer, large, white, in heads on long stem 1 to 1.5 long. **Plate 151**
Dianella caerulea: A straggling plant with group of strap-like leaves at end of slender stem 60 to 90 cm long; flowers in spring, light blue with yellow

stamens on slender stems, followed by shiny purple berries.
Dianella tasmanica: a tufted plant with greyish-green, folded, strap-like leaves 30 to 40 cm; flowers in spring, pale blue with yellow stamens, on slender stems.
Diplarrena moraea: a tufted plant, 30 cm, with a number of smooth, tapered, strap leaves; flowers in spring, white with yellow, with 3 spreading petals at end of stem.
Orthrosanthus multiflorus (Morning Iris): a clump-forming plant with soft, greyish-green, strap leaves 30 to 40 cm; flowers pale blue in spring, on long slender stems to 90 cm. **Plate 141**
Patersonia glabrata (Native Iris): a tufted plant with dark green, strap leaves about 30 cm long; flowers in spring, mauve, with 3 large petals at end of stem 30 cm long. **Plate 147**
Patersonia occidentalis (Native Iris): a tufted plant with greyish-green, narrow, strap leaves 25 to 30 cm long; flowers in spring, lilac, with 3 large petals at end of stem to 95 cm.
Sowerbaea juncea: a tufted plant with numerous narrow, grass-like, green leaves to 25 cm; flowers small, mauve, in heads on stems to 25 cm. **Plate 143**
Stylidium graminifolium (Trigger Flower): a tufted plant with crowded, stiff, narrow leaves 8 to 25 cm long; flowers in spring and summer, small, pink, in groups at tip of slender stem to 30 cm.
Stypandra caespitosa: a tufted plant with numerous, narrow, greyish-green leaves to 25 cm; flowers purple, in spring, in clusters at end of slender stems to 25 cm.
Stypandra glauca: an erect to straggling plant 60 cm or more with long, greyish green stem clasping leaves; flowers blue in clusters at end of slender stalks in spring. **Plate 146**
Thysonotus multiflorus (Fringe Lily): a tufted plant with numerous, narrow, greyish-green leaves 20 to 30 cm; flowers mauve, with finely fringed petals, in heads on stems to 30 cm in spring. **Plate 145**

F: Climbing and Creeping Plants

Billardiera cymosa (Sweet Apple Berry): a slender, stiff, twining plant with oblong leaves, silky when young; flowers in spring, tubular, with spreading lobes, creamish to bluish, in small clusters.
Billardiera erubescens: a climbing plant with dark green, leathery, elliptical leaves; flowers in spring, bright red, tubular, in small clusters.
Billardiera longifolia (Purple Apple Berry): a twining plant with narrow, elliptical leaves; flowers in spring, tubular, yellowish-green, followed by shiny purple berries.
Billardiera scandens (Apple Berry): a slender, twining plant with oblong shaped leaves; flowers in spring, greenish-yellow, tubular, with spreading lobes.
Chorizema diversifolia: a very slender, twining plant with lance shaped leaves; flowers reddish-orange, pea shaped, in spring.
Cissus antarctica: a vigorous climbing plant, with broad, heart shaped, toothed leaves; flowers tiny, in spring—a useful indoor plant.
Cissus hypoglauca: a vigorous climbing plant with greyish-green leaves divided into 5 spreading leaflets; flowers tiny, in spring—a useful indoor plant.
Clematis aristata (Old Man's Beard): a climbing plant with 3-lobed, toothed, heart shaped leaves; flowers in spring, white and starry, followed by bearded seeds on female plants. **Plate 158**
Clematis glycinoides: similar to *C. aristata*. Flowers smaller, leaflets less toothed, more suitable for shaded position.
Clematis microphylla: a climbing to ground-spreading plant; leaves with 3 narrow leaflets; flowers in spring, creamish.
Hardenbergia comptoniana (Native Wisteria): a vigorous twining plant, leaves with 3 lance-shaped leaflets, bluish-purple pea flowers, in sprays, in spring. **Plate 158**
Hardenbergia violacea (False Sarsparilla): a twining to erect growing plant with lance to egg shaped leaves; small purple pea flowers in sprays during spring. **Plate 159**
Hibbertia dentata: a twining plant with soft, oval, toothed, rough leaves; flowers in spring, large, bright yellow. **Plate 156**
Hibbertia scandens: a vigorous twining plant with smooth, soft, oval leaves; flowers in spring, very large, bright yellow.
Hoya australis: a slender twining plant with fleshy, shiny, oval leaves; flowers in spring and variable times, small, waxy, white with reddish centres, in clusters.
Kennedia beckxiana: a twining plant with smooth, greyish-green leaves with 3 leaflets; long, red

pea flowers with a greenish-yellow base, in pairs, during spring.

Kennedia coccinea (Coral Vine): a twining plant with dark green leaves with 3 round leaflets; small orange-red pea flowers in clusters, in spring.

Kennedia macrophylla: a vigorous twining plant, leaves with 3 large round leaflets; small, orange-red pea flowers in clusters in spring.

Kennedia nigricans: a vigorous twining plant, leaves with 3 smooth round leaflets; long yellow flowers with a black base, in spring.

Kennedia rubicunda (Red Bean): a vigorous twining plant, leaves with 3 lance shaped leaflets; large, deep red pea flowers in pairs, in spring.

Pandorea jasminoides (Bower Plant): a vigorous twining plant; leaves dark green with shiny leaflets; flowers in spring and summer, large, white, tubular, with red throat.

Pandorea pandorana (Wonga Wonga): a vigorous twining plant; leaves with a number of coarse leaflets; flowers in spring, tubular, cream with red throat—selected forms with white or yellow flowers.

Passiflora cinnabarina (Red Passionflower): a climbing plant with 3-lobed leaves; flowers large, red, in spring. **Plate 152**

Sollya heterophylla: a twining bushy plant; leaves oblong, dark green; flowers in spring, blue, in clusters—also white and pink forms. **Plate 157**

G: Prostrate-type Plants

(suited to baskets and hanging containers)

Ground Hugging Herbaceous Trailing Types

Dampiera diversifolia: a plant with soft trailing stems and small, lance shaped leaves; flowers in spring, blue to purple with white base.

Goodenia hederacea: a spreading plant with soft trailing stems, round to ivy shaped leaves; flowers in spring, yellow, with petals in a one sided manner.

Hemiandra pungens: a vigorous spreading plant with trailing stems and narrow pointed leaves; flowers in spring, pink, tubular with red-spotted throat. **Plates 1, 137**

Isotoma fluviatilis: A soft mat-forming plant with thin stems rooting freely, leaves small, light green; flowers spring and summer, small, pale blue.

Mazus pumilio: a close mat-forming fleshy plant with light green oval leaves; flowers in spring, small, pink with spreading lobes.

Mimulus repens: a soft mat-forming plant with slender trailing stems and small, egg shaped leaves; flowers in spring, small, pink with spreading lobes.

Myoporum debile: a spreading plant with trailing stems and fleshy, lance shaped leaves; flowers chiefly spring, white, small, bell shaped, followed by shiny pink to reddish berries. **Plate 136**

Phylla nodiflora: a mat-forming plant with fleshy stems and greyish-green, round to oval leaves; flowers in spring and summer, tiny, pink with a number forming a globular head. **Plate 73**

Scaevola humilis: a mat-forming plant with soft trailing stems and soft, light green, oblong to oval leaves; flowers in spring and summer, pale blue with spreading lobes. **Plate 2**

Scaevola ramosissima: a scrambling plant with dark green, fleshy, hairy, coarsely toothed leaves; flowers in spring, large, violet, with spreading petals.

Viola hederacea (Native Violet): a soft, close, mat-forming plant with dark green, ivy-shaped leaves; flowers chiefly in spring, purple with white.

Wahlenbergia gloriosa: a suckering, spreading plant with soft, dark green, round to spoon shaped leaves; flowers in summer, deep purple to violet.

Low Growing Mat to Cushion-like Types

Brachycome aculeata: a suckering daisy with soft, round to wedge shaped, coarsely toothed leaves; flowers in spring to summer, blue to pink petals, yellow centre.

Brachycome angustifolia: a suckering daisy with soft, narrow leaves; flowers over an extended period, blue to pink petals and yellow centre.

Brachycome ciliaris: a cushion-forming daisy with soft, divided leaves; flowers over an extended period, blue to pink petals and yellow centre. **Plate 133**

Brachycome multifida: a cushion-forming daisy with soft, crinkly, divided leaves; flowers over an extended period, blue to pink petals and yellow centre.

Brachycome stuartii: a close cushion-forming daisy with closely divided, soft leaves; flowers over an extended period, blue petals and yellow centre. **Plate 6**

Correa decumbens: a low growing, spreading plant, with oblong to elliptical leaves; flowers late spring, tubular, red with green apex.
Dampiera hederacea (Karri Dampiera): a straggling, spreading, sometimes suckering plant, with fleshy, ivy shaped leaves; flowers in spring and early summer, blue, with spreading petals.
Frankenia pauciflora: a cushion-forming plant, with slender stems and small, oval, greyish-green leaves; flowers in spring, small, pink.
Hibbertia diffusa: a prostrate spreading plant, with round leaves, slightly toothed at apex; flowers in spring, large, bright yellow. **Plate 134**
Hibbertia obtusifolia: a plant somewhat resembling *H. diffusa* but leaf edges entire.
Hibbertia pedunculata: a spreading plant with numerous small oval leaves; flowers in spring, bright yellow, on slender stalk.
Hibbertia stellaris: a cushion-forming plant with soft reddish stems and narrow leaves; flowers in spring, numerous, orange. **Plates 7, 66 and cover**
Hibbertia vestita: a spreading plant with small, fleshy, light green, narrow, oval leaves; flowers over an extended period, bright yellow. **Plate 138**
Kennedia eximia: a prostrate plant with leaves of 3 round leaflets; flowers in spring, red, pea shaped.
Pultanaea pedunculata: a spreading plant with numerous, small, oval leaves; yellow with red pea flowers in spring.
Rulingia hermaniifolia: a prostrate plant with rough, crinkled, oblong to lance shaped leaves; flowers in spring, small, white, with spreading petals. **Plate 54**
Scaevola striata: a spreading plant with soft stems and fleshy, dark green, oblong to lance shaped, coarsely toothed leaves; flowers in spring, violet, large, fan-shaped.
Scleranthus biflorus (Cushion Plant): a dense cushion-forming moss-like plant with numerous, narrow, light green leaves; flowers in spring, small, white.

H: Large Spreading-type Plants

Grevillea biternata: a very vigorous, prostrate and erect growing plant with light green, divided leaves; flowers in spring, white, in clusters. **Plate 46**
Grevillea* x *gaudichaudii: a prostrate spreading plant with trailing reddish stems and leathery lobed leaves; flowers in spring, reddish-purple, in one sided sprays.
Grevillea juniperina (prostrate form): a prostrate spreading plant with narrow, pointed, light green leaves; flowers in spring, yellow, in clusters.
Grevillea laurifolia: a prostrate wide-spreading plant with leathery oval leaves; flowers in spring, reddish, in one sided sprays.
***Grevillea* 'Royal Mantle':** a vigorous spreading plant, similar to *G.* x *gaudichaudii*.
Grevillea thelemanniana (prostrate form): a spreading shrub with greyish-green, divided leaves; flowers in spring, red, in one sided sprays. **Plate 139**
Homoranthus flavescens: a spreading shrub with narrow, fleshy, greyish-green leaves; flowers in spring, yellow in pincushion-like heads.
Kennedia prostrata (Travelling Postman): a wide-spreading, prostrate plant with slightly hairy, greyish-green leaves; flowers in spring, bright red, long, pea shaped. **Plate 140**
Micromyrtus ciliata: a spreading shrub with numerous, very small, narrow leaves; flowers in spring, small, white, star shaped. **Plate 94**
Scaevola aemula: a soft, bushy, spreading shrub with light green, oblong to oval, coarsely toothed leaves; flowers in spring, pale mauve with yellow base. **Plate 138**

I: Eucalyptus
(small growing, coloured, flowered types)

Eucalyptus caesia (Silver Princess): a small pendulous tree, 2 to 3 m, with powdery branches, leaves and flower buds; flowers winter and spring, large, pink to red stamens with large seed pods.
Eucalyptus forrestiana (Fuchsia Gum): a small erect tree, about 2 m, with narrow, lance shaped leaves; flowers summer to autumn, yellow stamens, flower buds large, pendulous, 4-winged, red to orange-red.
Eucalyptus grossa (Coarse-leaved Mallee): a small mallee to 2 m with thick, shiny, broad, heart shaped leaves; flowers spring, red flower buds and yellow stamens.

Eucalyptus leucoxylon "Rosea": a small tree, about 3 m, with leathery, lance shaped leaves; flowers chiefly autumn, bright red, in clusters.
Eucalyptus macrocarpa (Mottlecah): a sprawling shrub, 1 to 2 m, with large, silvery-grey leaves; flowers chiefly winter to spring, with large grey flower buds and long crimson stamens.
Eucalyptus preissiana (Bell-fruited Mallee): a small spreading shrub, 1 to 2 m, with thick, lance shaped leaves; flowers winter to spring, large buds and bell shaped fruit, stamens bright yellow.
Eucalyptus pyriformis (Pear-fruited Mallee): a small spreading mallee, 1.5 to 2 m, with small, lance shaped leaves; flowers winter to spring; large pear shaped buds and fruit, stamens yellow to red.
Eucalyptus rhodanthe (Rose Mallee): a straggling mallee, 1.5 to 2 m, with large, silvery-grey leaves; flowers various times, large-stalked grey flower buds and long, usually crimson, stamens.
Eucalyptus tetraptera (Square-fruited Mallee): a spreading, straggling mallee, 1 m or more, with thick, lance shaped leaves; flowers autumn to winter; large, square, ridged fruit and red buds, stamens pink to red.
Eucalyptus torquata (Coral Gum): a small tree, 2 to 3 m, with lance shaped leaves; flowers spring and summer; flower buds ribbed with pointed cap, stamens pink to red; flowers produced when plant is quite small.

Grey Foliaged Leaf Types (may be kept small by cutting foliage)

Eucalyptus cinerea (Argyle Apple): a bushy tree with opposite stem-clasping, grey, heart-shaped leaves; small cream flowers in summer.
Eucalyptus globulus (Tasmanian Blue Gum): a large tree producing juvenile, opposite, broad, blue grey stem-clasping, long, egg-shaped leaves; mature leaves large, dark green, lance-shaped; white flowers not produced with juvenile foliage.
Eucalyptus gunnii (Cider Gum): a medium sized tree with juvenile, small, round to heart-shaped, opposite, grey leaves; mature leaves lance-shaped; juvenile leaves are maintained by cutting foliage; flowers white.
Eucalyptus kruseana (Book-leaf Mallee): a straggling mallee to 2 m with round, opposite, stem-clasping, bluish grey leaves; flowers in winter, small, pinkish buds, yellow stamens.
Eucalyptus perriniana (Spinning Gum): a small straggling mallee with grey opposite juvenile leaves joined together at base, old leaves become detached and form discs which rotate in the wind; mature leaves lance-shaped.
Eucalyptus pulverulenta (Powdered Gum): a small spreading tree, with opposite, silvery grey, heart-shaped leaves; white flowers in spring.

J: Foliage Plants

(for shaded areas and for indoor use for limited periods)

Acmena smithii: a small bushy tree, 3 m, with shiny, dark green, oval leaves with an extended point; flowers in spring, fluffy, white, followed by cream to purplish berries.
Araucaria cunninghamii (Hoop Pine): a tall growing conifer with dark green, fine, pointed leaves.
Araucaria heterophylla (Norfolk Island Pine): a tall symmetrical conifer with fine, crowded leaves.
Backhousia citriodora: a bushy tree, 3 m, with oval, lemon-scented leaves; flowers summer, cream.
Brachychiton acerifolium (Flame Tree): a slow-growing tree, with large, light green, lobed leaves; flowers in late spring, red.
Castanospermum australe (Black Bean): a bushy tree, 4 m, with large, shiny, dark green leaves with oval leaflets; flowers in autumn, red clusters.
Ceratopetalum apetalum (Coachwood): an erect tree with broad, elliptical, dark green leaves; flowers in spring, white, followed by fruit with extended reddish calyx.
Cissus antarctica: see Climbing and Creeping Plants, page 72.
Cissus hypoglauca: see Climbing and Creeping Plants, page 72.
Cordyline rubra: see Palm-like Plants, page 71.
Cordyline stricta: see Palm-like Plants, page 71.
Emmenosperma alphitonioides (Bonewood): a medium sized tree with dark green, shiny, broad, elliptical leaves; flowers yellow, in spring, followed by orange berries. **Plate 131**
Eupomatia laurina (Bolwarra): a bushy, spreading plant, 2 m, with shiny, long, broad, lance shaped leaves; new growth reddish-brown; flowers white, in spring.
Ficus benjamina (Weeping Fig): a spreading tree with pendulous branches and shiny, dark green, elliptical leaves with an extended end; flowers inconspicuous. **Plate 20**

Ficus hillii: a large spreading tree with shiny, dark green, elliptical leaves; flowers inconspicuous.

Ficus rubiginosa (Port Jackson Fig): a spreading tree with broad, dull green, elliptical leaves, brownish beneath; flowers inconspicuous.

Glochidion ferdinandi (Cheese Tree): a spreading tree with shiny, lance shaped leaves, arranged in a somewhat pinnate manner; flowers inconspicuous, followed by flat circular fruit.

Grevillea robusta (Silky Oak): an erect, bushy tree with large, divided, light green leaves; flowers in spring, orange, in one sided spikes.

Hicksbeachia pinnatifolia (Monkey Nut): a small tree with very large, tough, leathery, deeply lobed, toothed leaves; flowers in late spring, red, in spikes, followed by red fruit.

Howea fosterana (Kentia Palm): see Palms and Palm-like Plants, page 78.

Lepidozamia peroffskyana: see Palms and Palm-like Plants, page 78.

Livistona australis: see Palms and Palm-like Plants, page 78.

Macadamia integrifolia (Bush Nut): an erect, bushy tree with tough, long, broad, dark green leaves; flowers in spring, cream, in long sprays, followed by hard fruit. **Plate 123**

Macadamia tetraphylla: similar to *M. integrifolia*, but leaves toothed and in groups around stem; flowers mauve.

Macrozamia communis (Burrawang): See Palms and Palm-like Plants, page 78.

Pittosporum rhombifolium: an erect bushy tree, with shiny, green, toothed, rhomboid shaped leaves; flowers in spring, cream, bell shaped, in clusters, followed by orange berries.

Pittosporum undulatum (Native Daphne): a bushy, spreading tree with shiny, dark green, wavy, elliptical leaves; flowers in spring, cream, bell shaped, followed by orange berries.

Schefflera actinophylla (Umbrella Tree): an erect tree with large leaves divided into a ring of leaflets; flowers red, in autumn, winter.

Stenocarpus sinuatus (Fire-wheel Tree): a slow-growing tree with shiny leaves, entire or lobed at ends; flowers red, in autumn. **Plate 132**

Syzygium coolminianum: an erect, bushy tree with shiny, long, dark green, lance shaped leaves; flowers white, in spring, followed by bluish-purple fruit.

Syzygium crebrinerve: an erect, bushy tree with broad, dark green, oval leaves with an extended end; flowers white, in spring, followed by reddish-purple fruit.

Syzygium luehmannii: an erect, bushy tree with small, oval, shiny leaves and reddish new growth; flowers white, in spring, followed by red fruit. **Plate 24**

Syzygium paniculatum (Brush Cherry): an erect, bushy tree with narrow, egg shaped, shiny leaves; flowers white, in spring, followed by red fruit.

Syzygium wilsonii: a bushy, pendulous plant with dark green, long, broad, elliptical leaves; new growth red and pendulous; flowers in spring, red, in large clusters. **Plate 128**

Tristania conferta: a large tree with broad, dark green, elliptical leaves; flowers white, in summer.

Tristania laurina (Water Gum): a bushy, small tree with dark green, shiny, lance shaped leaves; flowers yellow, in summer. **Plate 121**

K: Ferns

(more easily grown types for protected positions)

Adiantum aethiopicum (Common Maidenhair Fern): a spreading plant with slender black stems and soft round leaflets.

Asplenium australasicum (Bird's Nest Fern): a plant which can become very large, with broad entire fronds arising from a central section.

Asplenium bulbiferum (Mother Spleenwort): a plant with a number of much divided fronds arising from a central section; producing small plants on fronds. **Plate 29**

Blechnum nudum (Fishbone Water Fern): a plant producing a number of broad, symmetrical fishbone fronds, arising from a central section.

Cyathea cooperi (Tree Fern): a quick-growing tree fern with large soft fronds and straw-coloured scales at base of fronds. **Plate 30**

Darvallia pyxidata (Haresfoot Fern): a creeping fern with soft, brown, hairy stems and light green, feathery fronds; ideal for baskets. **Plate 28**

Dicksonia antarctica (Soft Tree Fern): a large-growing tree fern with numerous long fronds and soft brown hairs at the base.

Doodia aspera (Prickly Rasp Fern): a tufted fern with rough, broad, fishbone fronds, with short, creeping stems forming new plants.
Pellaea falcata (Sickle Fern): a creeping fern with numerous shiny, dark green, fishbone fronds.
Platycerium bifurcatum (Elkhorn): a large-growing plant with green and brown basal sheathing fronds and forked lobed fronds.

L: Orchids

Easily Grown Epiphytic Types

Dendrobium* x *delicatum: a clump-forming plant with stems 25 to 30 cm and several lance shaped leaves at apex; flowers in spring, white, cream to pink, in slender sprays.
Dendrobium gracilicaule: a clump-forming plant with slender stems 25 to 30 cm and several lance shaped leaves at the apex; flowers in spring, yellow to greenish-yellow, in short slender sprays.
Dendrobium* x *gracillimum: a clump-forming plant with long stems 30 to 45 cm and several lance shaped leaves at the apex; flowers in spring, bright yellow, in slender sprays.
Dendrobium kingianum (Pink Rock Orchid): a clump-forming variable plant with stems 10 to 25 cm and several lance shaped leaves at the apex; flowers in spring, pink, red to white, in slender sprays. **Plates 31, 35**
Dendrobium lingueforme (Tongue Orchid): a creeping plant with thick oval leaves; flowers in spring, white, in short sprays. **Plates 10, 32**
Dendrobium speciosum (Rock Orchid): a large clump-forming plant with thick stems 25 to 30 cm long and large lance shaped leaves at apex; flowers in spring, cream to yellow, in long sprays. **Plate 39**
Dendrobium speciosum* var. *hillii: a large clump-forming plant with long stems 45 to 60 cm long and large, lance shaped leaves at apex; flowers in spring, cream, in dense long sprays. **Plate 33**
Dendrobium teretifolium (Pencil Orchid): a slender, creeping orchid with long, pendulous, slender, pencil-like leaves 25 to 30 cm long; flowers in spring, white with brownish markings in short pendulous sprays. **Plate 39**
Dendrobium hybrids: a number of *Dendrobium* hybrids have been developed. *Dendrobium* x *specio-kingianum* (also known as *D.* x *delicatum*) is an easily grown hybrid and has different forms, two of which, "Helen" and "Marie", shown in colour plates, are

A specimen plant of *Dendrobium* x *specio-kingianum* 'Marie' showing the shallow plastic seed tray in which it is growing.

vigorous, clumpforming types with pink flowers, stems to about 25 cm and several lance shaped leaves. **Plate 34**

Orchids for a Moist Protected Position

Sarcochilus falcatus (Orange Blossom Orchid): a small plant with flat, fleshy, lance shaped, often curved leaves; flowers in spring, white with yellow, with a few in a spray.
Sarcochilus fitzgeraldii (Ravine Orchid): a clump-forming plant with fleshy-curved, channelled leaves; flowers in spring, white to pink with red centre, in short sprays. **Plate 37**
Sarcochilus hartmanii: a clump-forming plant with fleshy, stiff, channelled leaves; flowers in sprays, white with red centre, in short sprays. **Plate 38**

Terrestrial Types for a Protected Position

Calanthe triplicate (Christmas Orchid): a clump-forming plant with very large, fluted, lance shaped leaves; flowers in midsummer, white, in group at end of long stem.
Phaius tancarvilliae (Swamp Orchid): a clump-forming plant with very large, fluted leaves; flowers in spring, large, cream with red and brown, in a spray at the end of a long stem.
Pterostylis curta (Greenhood): a small plant with soft leaves in a rosette at ground level; flowers in spring, green with white and brown, single at end of short stem.
Pterostylis nutans (Nodding Greenhood): a similar plant to *P. curta* but with flower bent forward.

M: Water Plants

Azolla pinnata: a small floating fern with feathery leaves, green in shade and red in full sun, growing rapidly over surface. **Plate 49**

Cotula coronopifolia (Water Buttons): a creeping bog or water plant with stem-clasping, lobed or entire, soft, light green leaves; flowers spring to winter, yellow, tiny, with a number forming a button-like head.

Marsilea angustifolia (Nardoo): a water fern with creeping stems and small, light green, 4-lobed, clover-like leaves. **Plate 53**

Marsilea drummondii (Common Nardoo): a water fern with creeping stems and woolly, greyish, 4-lobed, clover-like leaves. **Plate 51**

Marsillea hirsuta (Nardoo): a water fern with creeping stems and light green, 4-lobed, clover-like leaves.

Nymphoides germinata (Wavy Marshwort): a water plant with small, round to heart shaped, light green, floating, water-lily leaves; flowers in spring, bright yellow, with 5 spreading fringed petals. **Plate 50**

Nymphaea gigantica (Water Lily): a water plant with large, round floating leaves; flowers pink to blue in large rosettes; for large troughs and tubs.

Rununculus rivularis: a creeping bog or water plant with circular to heart-shaped, finely dissected leaves; flowers in spring, small, shiny, pale yellow.

N: Palms and Palm-like Plants

(These plants require a plentiful supply supply of water)

Archontophoenix cunninghamiana (Bangalow Palm): a tall palm with a crown of large leaves with long smooth leaf bases; leaflets arranged in feather-like manner; flowers late summer, pale blue, in pendulous branched sprays.

Archontophoenix alexandrae (Alexander Palm): similar to *A. cunninghamiana* but leaflets greyish beneath, flowers cream; less cold tolerant.

Cordyline rubra: an erect plant 1 to 2 m, with large long, lance-shaped, stem-clasping leaves, clustered at the upper ends of stems in older plants; flowers in spring, mauve, in branched sprays. **Plate 150**

Cordyline stricta: an erect plant 1 to 2 m, with large long, narrow, stem clasping leaves, clustered at upper end of stem in older plants; flowers in spring, mauve, in branched sprays.

Cycas media: a very slow growing palm-like, non-flowering plant, with a crown of large stiff leaves, thorny leaf stalks and numerous narrow-veined leaflets.

Howea fosterana (Kentia Palm): a tall slender palm with a crown of large leaves, leaflets shiny and arranged in a feather-like manner; flowers tiny, cream, in a pendulous spike.

Lepidozamia peroffskyana: a very slow growing palm-like plant with a crown of large leaves divided into numerous shiny dark green leaflets, arranged in a feather-like manner. **Plate 22**

Livistona australis (Cabbage-tree Palm): a tall palm with a crown of large leaves with a thorny leaf stalk and broad fan-shaped blade. There are also a number of different *Livistona* species which are satisfactory if available. **Plates 23, 23a**

Macrozamia communis (Burrawang): a very slow growing palm-like plant, usually with an underground stem and a crown of large dark leaves, divided into numerous shiny leaflets.

O: Plants for Shaded Positions

The letter after the plant name refers to the list in which a full description will be found.

Part Shade

Acacia elata (C)
Acacia drummondii (C)
Bauera rubioides (C)
Bauera sessiliflora (C)
Boronia anemonifolia (C)
Boronia crenulata (C)
Boronia denticulata (C)
Boronia floribunda (C)
Boronia fraseri (C)
Boronis fraseri x *mollis* (C)
Boronia heterophylla (C)
Boronia megastigma (C)
Boronia mollis (C)
Boronia molloyae (C)
Boronia pinnata (C)
Boronia polygalifolia (A)
Boronia serrulata (C)
Brachycome aculeata (G)
Brachycome angustifolia (G)
Brachycome ciliaris (G)
Brachycome multifida (G)
Brachycome stuartii (G)
Chorizema cordatum (C)
Chorizema diversifolia (F)
Chorizema ilicifolium (C)
Correa aemula (C)
Correa bauerlenii (C)
Correa decumbens (C)
Correa "mannii" (B)
Correa pulchella (B)
Crowea exalata (C)
Crowea saligna (C)
Dampiera hederacea (G)
Epacris impressa (C)
Epacris longiflora (C)
Eriostemon nodiflorus (C)
Eriostemon spicatus (C)
Helichrysum elatum (C)
Hibbertia dentata (F)
Hibbertia diffusa (G)
Hibbertia obtusiflora (G)
Hibbertia pedunculata (G)
Hibbertia vestita (G)
Hovea acutifolia (D)

Hovea elliptica (D)
Hovea lanceolata (D)
Indigofera australis (C)
Olearia tomentosa (C)
Orthrosanthus multiflorus (E)
Passiflora cinnabarina (F)
Patersonia glabrata (E)
Patersonia occidentalis (E)
Pittosporum revolutum (D)
Plectanthus argentatus (B)
Prostanthera denticulata (B)
Prostanthera nivea (C)
Prostanthera nivea var. *induta* (C)
Prostanthera rotundifolia (D)
Rhododendron lochae (C)
Scaevola ramosissima (G)
Symphionema montanum (B)
Tetratheca ciliaris (A)
Tetratheca ericifolia (A)
Tetratheca thymifolia (A)
Viola hederacea (G)

Full Shade

Acmena smithii (J)
Araucaria cunninghamii (J)
Araucaria heterophylla (J)
Archontophoenix alexandrae (N)
Archontophoenix cunninghamiana (N)
Backhousia citriodora (J)
Brachychiton acerifolium (J)
Castanospermum australe (J)
Ceratopetalum apetalum (J)
Cissus antarctica (F)
Cissus hypoglauca (F)
Cordyline rubra (N)
Cordyline stricta (N)
Emmenosperma alphitonioides (J)
Eupomatia laurina (J)
Ficus benjamina (J)
Ficus hillii (J)
Ficus rubiginosa (J)
Glochidion ferdinandi (J)
Hicksbeachia pinnatifolia (J)
Lepidozamia peroffskyana (N)
Livistona australis (N)
Macadamia integrifolia (J)
Macadamia tetraphylla (J)
Macrozamia communis (N)
Pittosporum rhombifolium (J)
Pittosporum undulatum (J)
Stenocarpus sinuatus (J)
Syzygium coolminianum (J)
Syzygium cerebrinerve (J)
Syzygium luemannii (J)
Syzygium paniculatum (J)
Syzygium wilsonii (J)
Tristania conferta (J)
Tristania laurina (J)

Index

Numbers in *italics* are main text entries.